FIRSTFRUITS

Managing the Master's Money

Lillian V. Grissen FIRSTFRUITS

Acknowledgment

We are grateful to Rich Bishop, artist from Asheville, South Carolina, for creating the cartoons, and to Rev. Robert Heerspink, pastor of Cottonwood Heights Christian Reformed Church, Jenison, Michigan, for field-testing the course and offering helpful and creative suggestions for improvement.

ISBN 1-56212-019-0

9 8 7 6 5 4 3 2 1

Contents

Preface

God owns the universe, and by his acts of creation and redemption, he also owns us, his children. Our role as stewards of the world and its resources is the subject of *Firstfruits: Managing the Master's Money*, a biblically based stewardship program prepared by the Barnabas Foundation.

Increasingly, churches are experiencing difficulties in gathering gifts for ministry. Most people agree that giving grudgingly and sparingly rather than joyfully and generously robs God's people of the grace and blessing of true biblical stewardship. Yet little attention has been given to stewardship, and few congregations have been concerned about the need for *training* future generations to give. Giving often has not been emphasized as a *spiritual* exercise. Churches have only recently recognized that stewardship is a discipline *about which a body of knowledge exists*, and *in which people can and should be trained*.

The stewardship of money, an elementary form of stewardship, is mentioned in more than two thousand verses of Scripture and in nearly one-half of Christ's parables. This scriptural basis of stewardship is the emphasis of *Firstfruits: Managing the Master's Money*.

Firstfruits, a stewardship education project of the Barnabas Foundation, is indebted to many people who contributed their insights, time, and talents in developing these materials. I wish to acknowledge with deep appreciation the writing skills and personal concern of Lillian V. Grissen, former associate editor of *The Banner*. I also wish to acknowledge the encouragement of Stewardship Committee members and the guidance of Dennis Hoekstra, executive director of the Barnabas Foundation, in working toward completion of these materials.

Firstfruits will attempt to help churches in training their members to honor the Lord with their wealth, to give the firstfruits of their assets to God. Through a careful presentation of biblical stewardship principles, church members will learn how to be more productive in acquiring financial assets, more careful in using and conserving these assets, and more generous and joyful in distributing these material blessings to the ministries of the church.

With motivated denominational leadership, the preaching, teaching, pastoral, and diaconal work in our churches will lead to more effective and systematic attention to financial stewardship. May God bless these efforts, made on behalf of his people, so that all will experience the true joy of giving and sharing of that which belongs to God, that which is graciously entrusted to us as his stewards.

Dirk W. Vander Steen,
Director, FIRSTFRUITS

Introduction

If you could recall in detail all that you said and did during the past week, how many of your thoughts, actions, and decisions would be related to money? Try it and see.

If we're honest with ourselves, we have to admit that too much of what we think, say, and do revolves around money—or the lack of it. We in North America fidget at times about "making ends meet" and ignore the fact that we are the wealthiest people on earth. Astronomers who map out the form of our Milky Way galaxy and the structure of the universe see the earth as a small dot in the infinite sea of space. God sees not only our small planet but also the nearly four billion people on it. He sees that although he has placed sufficient resources on this planet to feed, clothe, and house everyone, humankind has distributed wealth inequitably.

It is time to listen again to God's call to good stewardship.

A Covenant of Friendship

Yours, O LORD, *is the greatness and the power*
and the glory and the majesty and the splendor,
for everything in heaven and earth is yours.
Yours, O LORD, *is the kingdom;*
you are exalted as head over all.
Wealth and honor come from you;
you are the ruler of all things.
In your hands are strength and power
to exalt and give strength to all.
Now, our God, we give you thanks,
and praise your glorious name.
—David's Prayer, 1 Chronicles 29:11-13 *Yancy, p. 229*

In these verses we find the two main elements of biblical stewardship: God as Creator-Owner, and humankind as grateful worshipers. God has a big part—the *biggest* part one can imagine. Compared to God, we have a very small role. Yet to perform our part well, to be the best stewards of God's property that we can, will require all of our effort, all of our lives—and we can do it only through God's grace.

Biblical stewardship is, in a sense, God's covenant (a binding agreement) of friendship with humankind. God became our friend and enabled us to be his friends (John 15:14). Within this friendship, God both offers privileges and impos-

7

es obligations. He promises and requires. He redeems from sin and frees to serve. Truly, we would not be able to be stewards for God if he had not given that ability to us in the first place.

God's Majesty

We people, egalitarian North Americans particularly, are so earthbound in our understanding of the word *majestic* that it is hard for us to comprehend the majesty of God. We use the word *majesty* to describe Mount Kilimanjaro, Victoria Falls, or the Grand Canyon. We might even describe as majestic the regal wedding of England's Prince Charles and Princess Diana.

But only when we grasp a tiny fraction of *God's* majesty can we even begin to appreciate the privilege of biblical stewardship. Who can say with Peter, "We were eyewitnesses of his majesty" (2 Pet. 1:16)? God's attributes—his holiness, love and compassion, splendor, and glory—are all parts of his majesty. So great is God's majesty that when he spoke the Ten Commandments, he put a limit-line around Mount Sinai. He told Moses to tell the people, "Whoever touches the mountain shall surely be put to death" (Ex. 19:12).

His Majesty is *our* God! Mysterious. Inexplicable. Unimaginable. The same God who created the infinite universe created males and females and told them to take care of planet earth. They in their pride tried to be like God, but, of course, they couldn't. With that first bite they knew they had ruined that perfect Creator-creature friendship.

You'd think the God of the universe might have shaken his head and chosen to start again on another planet; after all, he certainly had the opportunity; he knows each star by name (Ps. 147:4). But, no. This God of majesty, love, and mercy provided a way for male and female to be redeemed— to be restored in his sight. And when he renewed their lives with the promise of a Redeemer (Gen. 3:15), he again instructed them. Through this Redeemer, God enabled men and women to take care of his creation. Our task is to continue until our Redeemer returns.

God's Estate

When *Forbes* magazine publishes its annual list of the world's wealthiest, it consistently overlooks God. What an oversight! God's holdings extend as far as the universe. God's possessions include not only the assets encompassed by the *Forbes* list but also the "owners" of those assets. God owns not only tiny ants and giant rhinoceroses, but also babies still in their mothers' wombs and people who occupy palaces and White Houses.

God has not relinquished one smidgen or smithereen of his possessions. He has never transferred to people his ownership of certificates of deposit, nor his control of stocks and bonds, nor his title to all earthly real estate. He said "every animal of the forest is mine, and the cattle on a thousand hills" (Ps. 50:10). God, speaking through today's poet, might say, "all the diamonds in all the mines are mine, and all the gold in Fort Knox and other treasure houses are mine." And if there are planets in the universe where more people and more things exist, God owns them too.

God retains ownership—permanently. He "calls the shots"; he "holds the purse strings." We are merely "owners *pro tem*"—during the interim until he returns. Abraham demonstrated how costly this stewardship can be. He accepted without reservation that his precious son, Isaac, belonged to God. And until Abraham heard the angel of the Lord call him to stop, he continued his preparation to "sacrifice [Isaac] as a burnt offering as God had commanded." We sometimes find this story disturbing. How could he? we wonder. "What if God asked *me* to do this?" How easy it is to forget that God asked the same sacrifice of himself—that God gave his only Son, Jesus Christ, for us.

The knowledge that our "assets" belong to God should change our lives as it changed Abraham's. When we acknowledge God as Owner, every use of our money and other material possessions becomes a spiritual decision. It's not, "Lord, what must I do with my money?" but rather, "Lord, what may I do for you with your money?"[1]

---

[1]Although this study focuses on the stewardship of money, it will help us to understand that the scope of biblical stewardship also includes our time, talents, and care for God's creation.

God's Plumb Line

Harry Blamires (*The Christian Mind*, Servant Books, 1963) has said, "As a member of the Church, [the contemporary Christian] undertakes obligations and observations ignored by the non-Christian. As a spiritual being, in prayer and meditation, he strives to cultivate a dimension of life unexplored by the non-Christian. But as a *thinking* being, the modern Christian has succumbed to secularization."

With our mouths we confess that our frame of reference is God's holy Word. In practice we are so hemmed in, often unconsciously, with the world's criteria that we fail to consciously separate everyday reality from the eternal, what is his from what is ours. For millions, television has become *the* frame of reference. And television ignores the spiritual and deifies the secular. Shallow and shoddy situations are standard.

Malcolm Muggeridge, in his 1973 resignation speech as rector of the University of Edinburgh, pointed out that the highest aspiration of humanity is to *see* God (*The End of Christendom*, Wm. B. Eerdmans Publishing Company, 1980). Do we want to see? What do we see? When we let God out of our sight, it becomes easy for us to let him out of our hearts and minds as well.

When we are attentive, we *see* God "standing by a wall that had been built true to plumb, with a plumb line in his hand," and hear him say to Amos, "Look, I am setting a plumb line among my people Israel; I will spare them no longer" (Amos 7:7-8). Any amateur who has tried hanging wallpaper knows that without a plumb line to establish an absolutely accurate vertical line from ceiling to floor, the wallpaper and its pattern will be askew.

If we are "thinking Christians," as Blamires calls us, then it isn't intellectually hard for us to accept stewardship as a reasonable requirement of God. We hear this truth in church and we assent, sometimes a bit too vaguely. And in our reflective moments we gratefully recognize that God "stretched out the heavens and laid the foundations of the earth" (Isa. 51:13).

However, in practice, we tend to fit God into a human mold, with human abilities and yes, even human limitations. As such, consciously acknowledging God in our daily living as Owner of every single thing that we eat, drink, wear, or do is another matter.

10

God's plumb line, simply speaking, is the law. "If you love me," Jesus said, "you will obey what I command." He also said, "Love God with all your heart, soul, strength, and mind." And which of these does not touch our billfolds and checkbooks?

Perhaps too often our plumb line is our neighbor's standard of approval. How do others rate us? By the satellite TV dish in our yard or the camcorder in our closet? By the number of late model-year cars we drive? By our jobs or our education? By the name-brand clothes we wear? By our titles? By the beauty of our homes and our taste in furnishing them?

The story is told of a diplomat, the late Clare Booth Luce, who lived part-time in Phoenix, Arizona. A repairman who once came to restore the air conditioning in her home noticed workmen painting and papering a bedroom. About nine months later the repairman returned to the Luce home for other work. He found the same persons working in the same bedroom. "Not finished yet?" he joshed. "Oh, yes," replied one, "but Mrs. Luce is redoing the room. She's expecting the same guests and she doesn't want them to see the same decor."

We see things so differently than God sees. "'My thoughts are not your thoughts, neither are your ways my ways,' declares the LORD" (Isa. 55:8). When it comes to choices in government, economics, politics, industry, business, education, and recreation, God's way and humankind's ways are usually absolute opposites. That's why Jesus said we must choose: "No one can serve two masters. Either he will hate the one and love the other, or he will be devoted to the one and despise the other. You cannot serve both God and Money" (Matt. 6:24).

In humanity's way, humankind is central. In God's way, God is central. And that makes all the difference! We Christians spend our lifetimes learning just a little about God's ways. And, at times, God's way with money is especially tough to grasp completely.

God's Challenge

All Christians are stewards. We manage God's creation, his time, his talents, *and his money*. We are not, however, merely employees. Rather, God has graciously equipped us to be stewards—good ones. Jesus said, "I no longer call you servants [employees], because a servant does not know his master's business." We are God's friends, Jesus said, because "everything I have learned from my Father I have made known to you" (John 15:14-15).

When, in the beginning of recorded Bible times, God's creatures misunderstood the meaning of his relationship with them and took matters into their own hands, God had to reteach them what stewardship entailed. In the Old Testament, God instructed his people to tithe, to give 10 percent of their increase. Tithing is first mentioned in Genesis 14, when Abraham voluntarily gave Melchizedek, King of Salem (about whom we know only a little), a tenth of all the spoils of a war Abraham had just won. Later God commanded every Israelite to give to him a tenth of all that he or she earned (Num. 18, Deut. 12).

Tithing is a good place to begin biblical stewardship. Many people complain that tithing is too much; they cannot "afford" it. But they are wrong. God says, ". . . you rob me . . . Bring the *whole* tithe into the storehouse . . . ." And further, "Test me in this . . . and see if I will not throw open the floodgates of heaven and pour out so much blessing that you will not have room enough for it" (Mal. 3:8, 10).

The New Testament contains no specific law of tithing; rather, it implies that we should give more, not less! God's grace is more fully revealed in the New Testament, and we are blessed not only with the knowledge but also with the experience of this grace. God's grace is the source and the foundation for biblical stewardship. Paul, in instructing the Corinthians to give to the needy in Jerusalem, said, "On the first day of every week, each one of you should set aside a sum of money in keeping with his income" (1 Cor. 16:2). The apostle here inaugurated proportionate giving to replace tithing.

God and Us

What can we say about our God? Ultimately we bow low before him and say, "I know that my Redeemer lives!" The way we handle our money is correlated to our relationship with the Lord. God's grace is free, but it is never without results. God's graciousness in giving his all compels and energizes; we cannot help but produce the results that the Lord requires.

Herein lies the irony of biblical stewardship: Gratitude is voluntary, but God requires it. Because God demands it, he also enables us to be grateful. His grace is indeed a mystery, but it is for real. God asks no more than he entrusts to us, but, says Paul, "It is required that those who have been given a trust must prove faithful" (1 Cor. 4:2). The chapters that follow will show us how.

Lillian V. Grissen

1 God: Owner of the Universe

In the beginning God created the heavens and the earth.
—Genesis 1:1

I am God, your God . . . .
I have no need of a bull from your stall
or of goats from your pens,
for every animal in the forest is mine,
and the cattle on a thousand hills . . .
for the world is mine, and all that is in it.
—Psalm 50:7, 9-10, 12

Know that the LORD is God.
It is he who made us, and we are his;
we are his people, the sheep of his pasture.
—Psalm 100:3

Q. What is your only comfort
in life and in death?

A. *That I am not my own,*
but belong—
body and soul,
in life and in death—
to my faithful Savior Jesus Christ.

He has fully paid for all my sins with his precious blood,
and has set me free from the tyranny of the devil.
He also watches over me in such a way
that not a hair can fall from my head
without the will of my Father in heaven:
in fact, all things must work together for my salvation.

Because I belong to him,
Christ, by his Holy Spirit,
assures me of eternal life
and makes me wholeheartedly willing and ready
from now on to live for him.
—Heidelberg Catechism Q & A 1

Reflection: Who Is the Owner?

Once there was a young Chippewa woman who had had enough of the big city—the bright lights and "the flesh pots of Egypt." She decided to return to the more natural setting of a northern Canadian reserve. Life was simpler there.

But before she left (having become obedient to the laws of the white man), she gave three weeks notice to her employer, collected her last paycheck, and began to pack her belongings. What a job that turned out to be!

Pictures, bedding, rugs, clothes, china, books—box after box until they almost reached the ceiling of her living room. She could almost see the envious looks of her friends on the reservation!

She was so tired she fell asleep. And she dreamed that she had arrived on the banks of the great Red River with her big pile of boxes spread around her. There she waited for her brother, who would bring the canoe for her journey home.

Finally her brother arrived. At first he seemed a little surprised at her pile of belongings, but he said nothing. He just went to work, carefully loading box after box onto the canoe until it was nearly full. But the stack of boxes on shore seemed no smaller.

"Why didn't you bring a bigger canoe?" she wailed.

Her brother answered quietly, "It's the biggest canoe on the reservation. Besides, Grandmother said she was sure it would do."

At the mention of her grandmother, the young woman became very quiet. She suddenly remembered what her grandmother had said to her: "Remember, my dear one, that if, when you come home from your adventure in the big city, you have more things to move than can fill one canoe, then you will know that you have become greedy. You will know that you have left behind the sacred traditions of your elders and have accepted the white man's ways. You will have taken more than your share, and others will not have enough. Don't let that happen to you, my granddaughter."

In her dream the young woman's eyes filled with tears of shame. She had become greedy and had betrayed her trust—and suddenly she knew what she must do. Her grandmother need never know. She would give away all her extra belongings and return to the reservation with only what she could carry in one canoe.

And when she awoke, that is exactly what she did.

—Adapted from Leone Dueck Penner, "Too Much for One Canoe," *Women's Concerns Report*, No. 96, May-June, 1991, pp. 4-5.

Taking Inventory

Few of us have ever attempted to fit all of our belongings into one canoe—or even one pickup truck. In a society obsessed with things, most people are so busy gathering more and more belongings that they seldom stand back and take an honest look at their pile of boxes on the shore.

Imagine that late tonight a fire starts in your basement. Before the smoke alarms wake you and your family, the kitchen is nearly consumed. You rush to a neighbor's and dial 911, but by the time the fire trucks arrive, half of the house has burst into flames, and by the time the fire is finally doused, all that is left of your home and the belongings you spent twenty years acquiring is a smoldering pile of rubble.

Heartsick and miserable, you call the insurance company the next morning to report your loss. "We will need a list," they tell you. "Write down all of the things that you lost in the fire."

"That's easy," you say, and you begin listing your valuables with a great deal of energy. But by the time you're halfway through the fifth page, you realize what an enormous task this inventory is going to be. How will you ever remember all of the items you stacked in the attic, for example? You find you're even having trouble recalling the contents of the kitchen drawers and the living room shelves. Where did all of this stuff come from?

Like the young Chippewa woman, most of us are unaware of how many boxes we are accumulating. If we really had to take an inventory, we would probably discover that it would take hundreds of boxes in dozens of canoes to replace the things we currently own.

Truth with a Twist

The Bible has quite a bit to say about "ownership." And much of its message is in shocking contrast to everything our society preaches. Society says, "You are what you own."

The Bible's teachings on the subject are totally different: You don't own a thing. God owns you, the world, the universe, and everything in it. "Know that the LORD is God," Psalm 100 tells us. "It is he who made us, and we are his."

The idea of God owning everything, including our*selves*, isn't an easy one for many people to swallow in a society where property rights are hallowed and the right to free enterprise is carefully guarded. Yet the Bible spells it out unmistakably; we read that God says, "Everything under heaven belongs to me" (Job 41:11).

Imagine trying to list the people and things that belong to God! God is absolute Owner of *everyone*—from presidents, kings, queens, and dictators, to unborn babies in the wombs of their mothers; from servants as noble as Mother Teresa to the miserable beggar on the streets of India whom she tenderly helps to die with dignity.

God is also absolute Owner of every*thing* in the universe. The earth is God's pantry and warehouse. The pantry of grains, produce, meat, and milk and the warehouse of cloth-

If God owns everything I can tell those scientists what's
really on the planet Mars—his paperwork.

ing and resources for shelter and warmth are loaded. Not all people have the same access to that pantry and warehouse, however, as long as 5 percent of the population (North Americans) raid the resources and take 87 percent of the food, clothing, and materials for shelters stored there. That so many suffer because they do not have enough shames us.

God is sovereign. God has never transferred ownership of the creation to people, but has rather appointed us as managers. That means that although everything belongs to God, we are God's distributors. Because God is Owner, he is also Master. Only by grace does God allow us to temporarily "possess" and enjoy earth's treasures.

But It's Mine!

A television comedian once said, "You know, I discovered a Rolls Royce on Fifth Avenue in New York. Beautiful, it was. I loved it, so I took it. I figured it was mine because I discovered it."

Like that comedian, many of us live with the idea that possession is nine-tenths of the law—especially when it comes to our earthly possessions. We are proud of what *we* have earned and what *we* own. We often conveniently forget that the title on these goods is not in our name but in God's. Even though God allows us to "possess" much, he remains the Owner.

God's creative power—divine and unmatchable—is the reason for his dominion of the universe. "He's got the whole wide world in his hands." That's difficult for us, as members of American middle-class society, to understand. After all, the right to individual, even absolute ownership, is the cornerstone of our capitalistic system. It has been said, "Who holds the purse, calls the shots."

In a reverent sense, God's purse is completely and absolutely his. So, in everyday language, God may call the shots. And he does—with magnificence and grace. The more fully we comprehend who God is, the more we will understand that stewardship rests on grace.

Grace for Fallen Stewards

To get a more complete picture of the relationship between stewardship and grace, let's take a close look at salvation history.

When God had finished creating heaven and earth, he saw that all that he had made was very good. But someone was needed to care for that good creation. It was then that God said, "Let us make man in our image, in our likeness, and let them rule over the fish of the sea and the birds of the air, over the livestock, over all the earth, and over all the creatures that move along the ground" (Gen. 1:26).

So God created male and female in his image, and told them to rule over creation, and God gave man and woman the wherewithal to do this ruling (Gen. 1:28). God provided men and women with generous resources—and expected them to be good stewards of what they had been given. In less than one hundred words, God issued an executive order for all time for the management of creation. Sin, of course, marred this beautiful arrangement, but even here God had a plan. God's grace took over.

Grace is our *good* God's flawless *goodness*, his unconditional and inclusive love and mercy. It is this mercy, spontaneous and brimming with compassion, that has drawn us to God. Paul says, "For it is by grace you have been saved, through faith—and this not from yourselves, it is the gift of God" (Eph. 2:8-9). The perfect God, as Paul says in his letter to Timothy, "richly provides us with everything for our enjoyment" (1 Tim. 6:17).

Stewardship emerges from that wonderful grace of God. It is crucial to understand that stewardship does not come simply from *knowing* what the Word of God requires of us. We can use the Bible to prove almost anything we wish. A much deeper and exciting reason for being good stewards is that in Christian stewardship we express our gratitude for the *relationship* we have with God through the gift of his only Son, given for our salvation.

Living in that relationship opens our eyes to the principles of stewardship expressed in the Bible. We are new creatures in Jesus Christ, and gratitude is the new song we sing. We are motivated by a deep love within rather than from a law without. With God's *gift* to us, how can we not be grateful stewards who express our love for him?

How humbling it is to think that this *good* God entrusts us with his riches. Stewardship that springs from gratitude becomes a question of "How much *can* I give?" rather than "How much must I give?" Through our use, enjoyment, and generous sharing of earthly things, we receive a foretaste of heavenly treasures and can live richly within the framework of Christian stewardship.

In What Do We Trust?

Because our culture is so focused on money and the things it can buy, however, it's sometimes difficult to keep the whole idea of grace and stewardship in perspective. Money—along with such things as children, family, gambling, drugs, and sports—threatens to take first place in our lives. And, as a minister once commented, "Anything that comes between you and your God is your god."

How stunningly ironic that United States currency is minted with the motto "In God We Trust" on it. It might be more accurate to say, "In Money We Trust." Money is the dynamic that keeps the capitalistic system going. Paul (1 Tim. 6:10) teaches that "the love of money is a root of all kinds of evil." Money can be incredibly demanding; at times, almost all-consuming. Indeed, it very easily becomes our god rather than being a means to serve our God.

Because we belong to God and because we are made in God's image, we are commanded to live like God-images. God has given us our instructions (Gen 1:28), which Calvinists have generally called the "cultural mandate," and more than enough resources to care for each other and for creation. In a real sense each of us is like the president of a company, a ministry, or an agency. The president or administrator is responsible for all the purchasing, distribution, planning, production, and success of the organization. All of our actions must prove that our trust is in God alone.

The Right to Own

Once there was a man who served many years in prison for stealing a loaf of bread. When he finally was released, he became a priest. One day he noticed the two silver candlesticks were missing from the front of his church. "Ah," he said, "It must be the person who took them has a greater need of them than the church does."

Few of us could view a robbery with such compassion and understanding. We are, like the society we live in, very attached to our things. If someone were to come to us, point to one of our precious belongings, and say, "I want this" or even "I need this more than you do," we would object (in most cases) to giving up that belonging. "It's *mine*," many of us would reply.

Ironically, the more things we accumulate, the more difficult it often becomes to live with the tension between the biblical idea that God owns everything and our North American view of individual property rights. It's easy to begin thinking that it is our inalienable right to live just as well as (and even better than) others around us.

If we take an honest look at our attitude toward our belongings, most of us will face some uncomfortable questions. Are we ready to give up our claims and to "transfer" ownership to the rightful Owner? Are we ready to admit that our rights are always subject to God's rights? Are we ready to acknowledge that every time we use our "property" or spend our money, we are making a *spiritual decision?*

These are not easy questions to deal with—even for those of us who struggle seriously with the question of money, possessions, and comparative affluence. We sometimes feel guilty over the abundance of material blessings we enjoy in North America, but we are unsure what to do about it. We need help and grace to make the confession of 1 Chronicles 29:11-12:

> Yours, O Lord, is the greatness and the power
>   and the glory and the majesty and the splendor,
>   for everything in heaven and earth is yours.
> Yours, O Lord, is the kingdom;
>   you are exalted as head over all.

For Discussion

1. Although we often find it simple to acknowledge that God owns everything, reflecting that truth in the way we live is more difficult. How might *living* as if God owns everything influence

    - the way we grocery shop?
    - the presents we put under our Christmas trees?
    - the types of vacations we plan?
    - our giving?

2. In the early church, Christians shared everything with one another. No one had more than another, and no one was in need:

    > All the believers were one in heart and mind. No one claimed that any of his possessions was his own, but they shared everything they had . . . There were no needy persons among them. For from time to time those who owned lands or houses sold them, brought the money from the sales, and put it at the apostles' feet, and it was distributed to anyone as he had need.
    > —Acts 4:32, 34-35

    Compare the early church with the Christian church in North America today. Is the "common sharing" of the early church an ideal we should strive for? How would the attempt to be more like the early Christian church impact your congregation? Your community?

3. Earlier in the session we discussed the fact that North Americans, 5 percent of the world's population, use 87 percent of the world's goods. If we think of all the world's goods as belonging to God—all part of God's big pantry and warehouse—then it's difficult not to acknowledge that we've taken far more than our rightful share.
    Think of some specific things we can do as individuals and as a church to restore the balance God intended in creation, to work toward a world in which everyone has enough.

4. How can we, as individuals and as families, distinguish between needs and wants? List some specific guidelines.

Think, Pray, and Do

Think

1. Read Isaiah 40:21-31, (praise for the Creator) and Job 37-41. These soul-stirring passages will help you appreciate the wonder of the creation and its Creator.

2. Think of two simple and practical things you can think or do that will help you *recognize* God's ownership.

Pray

1. Read the Meditation on page 25.

2. Use some of the following prayer suggestions:

   Praise: Praise God for creating the earth and heaven.
   Thanks: Thank God for the beauty of creating male and female to complement one another.
   Confession: Confess the pride we often have in things, which is really not so different from the sin of Adam and Eve.
   Petition: Request that we recognize that because God redeemed us from the bondage of sin we are *new* people.
   Intercession: Pray that the needs of others may become more real to us daily.

Do

1. List twelve large purchases that you made during the past year. Then try making them part of a confession that you can repeat throughout the week to help you remember that all of our possessions belong to God. For example:

   God, I know you own my new minivan.
   Lord, you've loaned me a warm winter coat, but all that I have belongs to you.

   And so on . . .

2. Check your last three annual income tax returns. Look at the amount of your charitable contributions. What percentage of your income did you give to church and charitable causes?

Meditation

Landlord Divine

In the beginning God created the heavens and the earth.
   —Genesis 1:1

Where were you when I laid the earth's foundation? Tell me, if you understand.
   —Job 38:4

He owns ranches and city lots, continents and islands, oceans and streams. All of them. Everywhere. He sells nothing—not his real estate, not his water or mineral rights. He charges no rent, offers no contracts, and grants no leases.

This amazing Landlord is God. Our God. We live on God's property, rent-free. At our disposal is his bank account of resources, from which we may and do borrow, interest-free.

This Landlord who owns the heavens and the earth and their abundant resources also created them. When God finished that matchless task, all the ingredients for Utopia were present. And God saw that it was good.

After this magnificent creation, God created humans. And seeing that male and female were good, God blessed them and put them in charge, commanding them to use and care for the entire creation (Gen. 1:28). God created you and me and everyone, with billions of different hearts, souls, minds, and strengths.

And we blew it. We spoiled everything. Permanently—almost. But, not wanting the creation nor those bearing his image to forever wallow in the damage they had done, this God, this Landlord Divine, intervened with the greatest resource of all: his love. Like the other resources, God's love is free. But that doesn't mean that no price had to be paid. The cost was awful. The English poet John Donne understood this; he described God as "that All . . . which cannot sin, and yet all sins must bear, which cannot die, yet cannot choose but die."

With that kind of love, God recreated humankind. God gave himself, through his Son Jesus Christ. "I am the Way," said Jesus. This gift—liberation, redemption, newness—enables us to take care of God's possessions, to be God's stewards. We are new people (Gal. 2:20); we are free (Gal. 5:1); we are loved (John 15:9).

"Tell me," says God, "if you understand."

Father God, we are speechless.

Prayer

Creator God of your world,
you have permitted us to live here,
with every need cared for.
Accept our praise
and our thanks.
We acknowledge that
the cattle on a thousand hills
belong to you and you alone.
We acknowledge that
the robins and the eagles
in the heavens
belong to you.
We acknowledge that
everything belongs to you.
We acknowledge that
we belong to you
and we are grateful.
We stumble a bit, Lord,
when you tell us
"The money in your billfold
belongs to me."
Forgive us, Father.
We falter, Lord,
when we see a neighbor's house
that is bigger or newer than ours.
Forgive us, Lord.
Open now our minds
and our hearts
so that you may teach us
to open our purses.
You gave all to us,
we want now
to give all to you.
We pray
in Jesus' name.
Amen.

2

Stewardship: God's Assignment

Each of you must bring a gift in proportion to the way the LORD your God has blessed you.
                                        —Deuteronomy 16:17

Take some of the firstfruits of all that you produce from the soil of the land the LORD your God is giving you and put them in a basket. Then go to the place the LORD your God will choose as a dwelling for his Name and say to the priest in office at the time . . . "and now I bring the firstfruits of the soil that you, O LORD, have given me."
                                        —Deuteronomy 26:2-3, 10

But when you give to the needy, do not let your left hand know what your right hand is doing.
                                        —Matthew 6:3

So do not worry, saying, "What shall we eat?" or "What shall we drink?" or "What shall we wear?" For the pagans run after all these things, and your heavenly Father knows that you need them. But seek first his kingdom and his righteousness, and all these things will be given to you as well.
                                        —Matthew 6:31-33

Freely you have received, freely give.
                                        —Matthew 10:8

On the first day of the week, each one of you should set aside a sum of money in keeping with his income . . . .
                                        —1 Corinthians 16:2

So we urged Titus, since he had earlier made a beginning, to bring also to completion this act of grace on your part. But just as you excel in everything—in faith, in speech, in knowledge, in complete earnestness and in your love for us—see that you also excel in this grace of giving.
                                        —2 Corinthians 8:6-7

God loves a cheerful giver.
                                        —2 Corinthians 9:7

Reflection: Nothing but the Best

Four-year-old Anjali squirmed in her seat. She had been running errands with her grandfather for over an hour, and she was sick of sitting in the car. She was impatient for movement and action. Before the car had come to a stop in the garage, Anjali loosened her seat belt. "The policeman can't see me here, can he, Grandpa?"

We may smile at this story of an impatient child and her notion of disobeying an authority who can't see her. But if we're honest with ourselves, we'll have to admit that Anjali's way of thinking is not just "kids' stuff." More and more adults in our society are living by a similar ethic: "If you can get away with it, it's all right."

Such a distorted sense of accountability is apparent even in the Christian church. People neglect their giving, fail to become involved, forget their responsibility to the poor and sick, and figure it's all right as long as no one points a finger at them. Their attitude is, "No one knows how much I give; few people keep track of how much I do—so I'll get by with the bare minimum." The truth is, of course, that even when our fellow church members don't object to poor stewardship, God demands better. With God, there is no "getting away with it."

In no way, of course, does our *giving* earn our salvation; our "accountability" has been taken care of by our Lord. But we are still responsible for the lives we live on earth. Paul, in 1 Corinthians 3:12-15, explains it best:

> If any man builds on this foundation using gold, silver, costly stones, wood, hay or straw, his work will be shown for what is, because the Day will bring it to light. It will be revealed with fire, and the fire will test the quality of each man's work. If what he has built survives, he will receive his reward. If it is burned up, he will suffer loss; he himself will be saved, but only as one escaping through the flames.

Not an Option

What exactly is involved in good stewardship? The following definition may be helpful:

Biblical stewardship is the productive and joyful acquiring, managing, using, giving, and sharing with others the very best—the firstfruits—of our time, talents, and possessions in the advancement of God's kingdom.

We cannot escape being stewards. We cannot choose whether or not we want to be stewards. We *are* stewards. We are obliged to be *good* stewards because God commands it and because he wants us to share of his bounties. And we *live as stewards* because we love our Lord.

Unfortunately, however, even though we all may try to live as good stewards, we are not always equally successful. For one thing, we do not all manage our money wisely. Some people are always broke, and others are always in debt. Consumer debt at the beginning of the 90s has reached almost $3 trillion. The business community owes another $3 trillion; the U.S. Government owes still another $3 trillion. The American people—and that includes you and me—have overspent their way into a debt of 9 trillion dollars!

For another thing, even when we do well at managing our finances, we are not always ready to share. We saw in chapter 1 how we in North America, only 5 percent of the world's population, use 87 percent of this earth's food, shelter, and clothing.

It's important to keep reminding ourselves that wisely managing and sharing our wealth are not options—that all we own and all we are able to own is a gift from God. As it says in Deuteronomy, "You may say to yourself, 'my power and the strength of my hands have produced this wealth for me.' But remember the LORD your God, for it is he who gives the ability to produce wealth" (Deut. 8:17-20).

It's also important to remember that stewardship is not a duty but a privilege. The Macedonians pleaded with Paul "for the *privilege* of sharing in this service to the saints" (2 Cor. 8:4). Full-time stewardship is our grateful response for all God's gifts to us.

The Old Testament tells us about Hannah, a woman who was deeply grateful for the privilege of sharing. Hannah prayed long and fervently for a son: "O LORD Almighty, if you will only look upon your servant's misery and remember me, and not forget your servant but give her a son, then I will give him to the LORD for all the days of his life . . ." (1 Sam. 1:11). God answered Hannah's prayer and gave her a son, and she responded in gratitude: "So now I give him to the LORD. For

29

his whole life he will be given over to the LORD" (1 Sam. 1:28).

We who may be third-, fourth-, and even fifth-generation Christians may have lost some of that early delight of salvation and the joy of looking for ways to express gratitude to God. Some of us may need to relearn how rewarding it is to be able to share our gifts and our money as well. In Luke 6:38 we read, "Give, and it will be given to you. A good measure, pressed down, shaken together and running over, will be poured into your lap."

How Should We Give?

It's not difficult to think of ways in which we should *not* give—grudgingly and unthinkingly, for example. But how *does* a faithful servant give? The following paragraphs will help define faithful giving.

Cheerfully

In 2 Corinthians 9:7 we read, "Each man should give what he has decided in his heart to give, not reluctantly or under compulsion, for God loves a cheerful [the word might even be translated *hilarious*] giver."

Most of us know what it feels like to give reluctantly, grudgingly, regretfully: We know we *should* pledge to the new

Stop trying to make change and just throw in the fifty-dollar bill.
You can survive a 10.05 % tithe.

Christian school drive, that it's expected of us, but in private we complain bitterly about this new strain on our budget. We read the council's guidelines for giving and groan. We pledge accordingly but in our hearts resent the church for taking so much.

That, says Paul, is not the kind of giving God requires of us. He wants us to give gratefully, eagerly—smiling as broadly as Ebenezer Scrooge did on Christmas morning when he found he still had a chance to give and to show love to others.

God wants us to give with hilarity, laughing and dancing in gratitude for grace. We give cheerfully, hilariously, because God has given so much to us.

Generously

Deuteronomy 16:17 tells us, "Each of you must bring a gift in proportion to the way the LORD your God has blessed you." Matthew 10:8 echoes that idea in the words, "Freely you have received, freely give."

Although most of us complain about the large bite inflation continues to take out of our paychecks, few of us are inclined to make significant changes in the types of goods and services we buy. We continue to eat out, buy our favorite name brands, and eat our favorite foods. It all costs more, sure—but we'd rather pay the ten or twenty dollars extra than give up something we enjoy.

That ten or twenty dollars that we dismiss quite easily at the checkout stand, though, often has a way of appearing much larger on Sunday morning when the offering plate is being passed around. When the deacons ask for our generous gifts for benevolence, hunger, or catastrophe, we give something—but it's usually not a ten- or twenty-dollar bill. It's usually a one-dollar bill—and has been for the past ten or twenty years. While we have gradually been required to pay more and more for a loaf of bread, a gallon of milk, and a gallon of gasoline during the past twenty years, no one has nudged us to make a comparable increase in our special gifts and offerings. So often we give our one-dollar gifts out of unthinking habit—regardless of need or inflation. As a result, a check of church records will undoubtedly indicate that giving has not kept apace with inflation. And that means many of us are doing a poor job of imitating God's generosity.

How do we break out of that bad habit? Someone has noted that one way of (temporarily, at least) surmounting our problems with static giving is to get rid of the one-dollar bill and replace it with the two-dollar bill. If people gave two-dollar bills instead of one-dollar bills, our offerings would double!

Quietly

"But when you give to the needy, do not let your left hand know what your right hand is doing," Jesus tells us (Matt. 6:3). We Christians often use this text as an excuse to keep our giving secret. After all, nothing is as private as our checkbooks. But is that the way it should be?

When Jesus talked about "quiet" giving, it's doubtful that he meant we should refrain from sharing with fellow Christians the joy of giving. Instead, he was warning us not to let our pride take over and make a display of our giving. In other words, Jesus meant, "Don't be a show-off! I know your heart. You can't bluff me!"

Upon returning from the Nigerian mission field because of the illness of the wife and mother, a needy young couple arrived home on a wintry January day. Some very good friends dropped in to greet them and to see how they could help. "Let us take care of the baby for you," they said. A bit later, the gentleman slipped an envelope into the father's hand. In the envelope was a hundred dollar bill—"for current expenses," he said.

These friends had learned to give from the heart—quietly, without show and without fanfare.

Selflessly

When Paul was in Corinth, he told the people there about the generosity of the church in Macedonia. He said, "Out of the most severe trial, their overflowing joy and their extreme poverty welled up in rich generosity. . . . they gave as much as they were able, and even beyond their ability. Entirely on their own, they urgently pleaded with us for the privilege of sharing in this service to the saints. And they did not do as we expected, but they gave themselves first to the Lord" (2 Cor. 8:2-5).

Here Paul points out the secret of giving: they gave themselves first to the Lord. The Macedonians provide an example we also may follow.

Wisely

During the past decade, television has brought us a host of evangelists whose "commercials" repeatedly ask for gifts. Although some of these evangelists do receive funds from Christians in the Reformed and Presbyterian traditions, most listeners are a bit skeptical of the repeated requests for money.

Once a year the magazine _The Other Side_ publishes a score-card of "Christian" organizations that use the mass media—TV, radio, magazines, and mass mailings—to collect funds. Included in the figures are the total income, the expenses, and an evaluation of how much of the money collected actually goes to the cause for which it was targeted. That score-card is discouraging. Some organizations have become an end in themselves.

We can be grateful that most of our churches are more responsible in their stewardship than these mass media ministries. The Christian Reformed Church, for example, practices good financial stewardship through an annual scrutiny of the agencies and organizations included in the "quota" (the annual amount expected of each CRC family to maintain all the approved agencies). This committee also scrutinizes and approves ministries that ask for special offerings.

God expects us to give wisely. This requires a thorough knowledge of the organizations to which we give.

What Should We Give?

The Bible tells us we should give our firstfruits back to God. Many of us, especially those raised in urban settings, may find that term "firstfruits" a little difficult to understand.

Exodus, Leviticus, and Deuteronomy speak of the firstfruits of the crops, the harvest of grain, the animals, wool, wine and oil. Psalm 78:51 even refers to the firstborn as firstfruits: "He struck down all the firstborn of Egypt, the _firstfruits_ of manhood." In the New Testament Paul said, "We ourselves . . . have the firstfruits of the Spirit" (Rom. 8:23).

Firstfruits are special. Enjoying their taste can be almost a spiritual experience—as one family in Phoenix, Arizona learned. The orange trees in this family's backyard started yielding fruit each year in December. But rather than rushing out to pick the fruit when it first ripened, the family waited to pick those first oranges until Christmas morning. For this family, those Christmas oranges symbolized the firstfruits given by the Father when he sent his only Son, Jesus Christ. And the first of the season's oranges were superb.

God wants to enjoy our firstfruits—our best and our most succulent. That means God doesn't want to settle for the left-over money that we might have, the time we squeeze out to pay homage to him, nor the leftovers of our talents.

Laraba was a patient at the Benue Leprosy Settlement hospital. She had been brought there by Anita Vissia from the Gidan Timaya Leprosy Clinic located near Lupwe, Nigeria, where the CRC had missionaries. Laraba knew the meaning of "firstfruits."

She had come to this hospital for surgery. When she arrived, she owned nothing, not even a completely intact body. Her fingers were gone; only stubby thumbs remained. She came hoping that doctors could perform reconstructive surgery to restore a walking surface to her toeless and hopelessly deformed feet.

As the superintendent of the Leprosy Settlement, I was able to visit Laraba frequently and witness her

More zucchini! Something tells me this program needs further clarification.

struggles. In spite of her many handicaps, Laraba did not give up. With her fingerless hands, she worked diligently on her embroidery as she recovered from surgery. With the needle held carefully between the stub of her thumb and the palm of her hand she would carefully, stitch by stitch, follow the pencil lines that I had traced on little pieces of cloth. Each cloth contained a different text or short proverb for her to embroider. Each little cloth took her weeks to complete.

On one occasion, when I was gone for several weeks on tour, I realized that I had not left any work for Laraba to do. When I returned, I expected a reprimand, but instead Laraba was smiling. With pain and care she had embroidered what she considered an English text for me. Guided by the writing on a bolt of cloth she could barely see in the corner of the room where she lay, she had embroidered, without the guidance of pencil lines, these words: "36" x 40 yards, Made in Czechoslovakia." How proud she was that she could thank me in my own language!

I thanked Laraba and said to her, "I simply cannot understand how you could make such a beautiful cloth for me." She lifted up her fingerless hands, and with some reprimand, said, "I make use of what I have."

She had given of her best, her firstfruits. It was a moment I will not forget.

—Dirk Vander Steen

Who's in Control?

Money is more than a medium that we use to exchange for things. It's one of the "things" God has given us to use, and of which he expects the firstfruits.

Representative Pat Schreuder, Colorado Democrat, once said, "Our lives are governed by the Internal Revenue Service." She probably could just as well have said, "Our lives are governed by money." A nineteenth-century poet put it differently: "Things are in the saddle and riding mankind." Many Christians may object to what Schreuder and the poet have said, but none of us are immune to the sneaky tricks money plays to subtly squeeze us in its greedy vise (or should we say vice?). Too often, our money manages *us*.

Two men met together after not having seen each other for twenty-five years. One of the men, a construction contractor, had become very wealthy; the other also was comfortably set. "Do you remember," said the first man to the contractor, "when we were young and we would say, 'I would be satisfied if I had my house paid for and $500 in the bank'? Do you still feel that way?" The contractor only grinned. The other continued, "Remember we used to sing that song, 'Take my silver and my gold; not a mite would I withhold'"?

"Yes," said the contractor, "but we never sing that verse anymore."

Often, like these two men, we sort of "drift" into a more comfortable lifestyle, seldom stopping to recognize how wealthy we have become. Because few of us tend to think of ourselves as rich, we may be tempted to look critically at our neighbor when we read Jesus' words in Matthew 19:24: ". . . it is hard for a rich man to enter the kingdom of heaven. Again I tell you, it is easier for a camel to go through the eye of a needle than for a rich man to enter the kingdom of God."

"Ah," you say, "I am not rich; I have a hard time making ends meet. With house payments, growing children, and Christian school tuition, there is very little left." In many of our families both parents work simply to pay the tuition.

God knows that and, in grace, never asks more of us than we can give. But God does ask us to look at our expenditures. A wise grandfather told his grandson and granddaughter-in-law, "It's not the high cost of living that gets us; it is the cost of high living." In comparison with most of the world, many of us are living high, and we are indeed rich.

Taking Stock of What We Have

Ron Blue, C.P.A. and managing partner of Ronald Blue & Co., an Atlanta-based financial planning and investment counseling firm, suggests that the three basic questions we must look at when we think about stewardship and money are these:

1. Do I have enough?
2. Will I ever have enough?
3. Will it continue to be enough?

Perhaps before we can honestly answer these questions, however, we need to decide just how much "enough" is. And for most of us that's tricky.

Some Christians struggle with guilt because they have so much. If we are sorry for our flaws and our sins, we need not struggle with guilt (for Christ has paid for that), but it is proper for us to rethink what we do with our money. It's appropriate for Christians to struggle with the questions of money and what we can do to correct the unfair distribution of it in the world today. We need to be ever alert to the King's commands.

The Heidelberg Catechism provides the premise and principle on our use of money as a spiritual gift:

Q. What do you understand by "the communion of saints"?

A. First, that believers one and all,
as members of this community,
share in Christ
and in all his treasures and gifts.

Second, that each member
should consider it a duty
to use these gifts
   readily and cheerfully
   for the service and enrichment
      of the other members.
                    —Heidelberg Catechism, Q & A 55

Money, most of us agree, is a "treasure," and it is also a "gift."

Once we have acknowledged the importance of sharing our money, the next question is "How much?" How much must we give? How much may we keep? For many years churches in the Reformed tradition have taught that stewardship means tithing, or giving 10 percent of our income. Tithing is important; the danger is that it can become legalistic rather than being an expression of our gratitude.

In the Old Testament, the tithe represented the legal requirement for fulfilling God's laws as stewards. God's people were *commanded* to give a tenth of everything they earned to further God's work.

The New Testament offers a new twist to the idea of stewardship—the idea of giving not only 10 percent, but giving our *all*. Look at the three words New Testament writers use to describe the role of a steward:

- *Pedagogos* (Gal. 3:24-25). A slave charged with the discipline and training of the master's children.
- *Epitropos* (Matt. 20:8; Luke 8:3). A slave charged with the responsibility of taking care of the master's estate.
- *Oikonomos* (Luke 12:42; 16:1, 3). A slave entrusted with the master's financial affairs.

In Greek homes stewards were highly valued servants entrusted with power and authority. They served out of love for their masters, but they were *slaves for life and never actually owned* anything. This analogy ought not to be overlooked for us as Christians in our steward-relationship with God.

Again and again, Jesus makes it clear that stewardship means giving our all. The clearest reason for this requirement is, of course, that Jesus Christ gave his all. He didn't have a home or a paycheck; he gave his life and his blood.

In the context of giving our all, managing our money becomes a serious responsibility for Christians. No longer may we go from paycheck to paycheck without thinking carefully about what we are doing with our money. We cannot use the gifts God gives us without considering carefully the ways in which our actions affect others.

In a sense we are not paid managers; but neither are we slaves. Remember, Jesus said, "You are my friends." We manage freely. We manage and care for the possessions God has given us as persons redeemed by grace.

Stewardship, then, is management; it is part of the firstfruits of a relationship created by grace. It is not governed by *laws* (you must do this and you must give that). It is governed by *grace*, the grace with which God has established his marvelous relationship with us.

True or False?

What does the Bible say about money?

_F_ 1. One out of every twenty verses in the gospels contains direct teachings on economic issues, such as the danger of wealth or a concern for the poor.

_f_ 2. In his teaching, Jesus addresses the subject of wealth and poverty more than he does any other subject.

_T_ 3. The Bible teaches that we cannot serve both God and Money.

_F_ 4. In the parable of the rich man and Lazarus, the rich man incurred the wrath of God because he was so wealthy.

_T_ 5. The statement that Jesus made, "It is easier for a camel to go through the eye of a needle than for a rich [person] to enter the Kingdom of God" (Matt. 19:24), refers to me.

_T_ 6. Our daily work, the acquisition and use of money, and the use of God's material blessings are deeply spiritual matters and ought to be honored among God's people.

_T_ 7. The mark of sacrificial giving in the New Testament is not how much is given, but how much is left after the giving is done.

_T_ 8. One of the sins for which Sodom was destroyed was the misuse of wealth and affluence.

_T_ 9. If money and wealth are obstacles to our total commitment to Christ, we should sell what we have and give it to the poor in order to follow Jesus.

_T_ 10. The New Testament, like the Old Testament, indicates that earning money by charging interest is legitimate and proper.

Bible Study

Read the Scripture assigned to your group. Then answer the two questions together and plan to report your findings to the larger group.

Group 1: Firstfruits

Read Deuteronomy 2:6, 10; Psalm 78:51; Romans 8:23.

Group 2: Talents

Read Matthew 25:14-30 and Luke 19:12-17.

Group 3: Giving

Read Deuteronomy 16:17; Matthew 10:8; 2 Corinthians 8:2-5; and 2 Corinthians 9:7.

1. What do these passages teach about stewardship?

2. Think of two or more implications these passages have for our personal giving.

Stewardship

Biblical stewardship is the productive and joyful acquiring, managing, using, giving, and sharing with others the very best—the firstfruits—of our time, talents, and possessions in the advancement of God's kingdom.

Anne's Story: A Case Study

What I struggle with is whether I can live *a* good life and *the* good life simultaneously.

It all seemed so much simpler when Phil and I were just married and in graduate school. Like the other graduate students we hung around with, we were perfectly happy in our rental apartments furnished with thrift store finds and relatives' castoffs. We all scorned everything middle class. We never watched TV, rarely used a car, loved to backpack, and baked our own bread.

We did everything naturally. But the natural birth control led to three kids real fast. Now Jared and Jacob are in first grade, and Jessica is in preschool. We're paying Christian school tuition for the kids, and we still haven't paid off all our school loans.

People can't understand why we panic sometimes. After all, Phil's a teacher, and I'm a free-lance accountant. But you know, kids are incredibly expensive! They need orthopedic shoes and tubes in their ears. They fall and knock out their new front teeth. And they lose a coat every winter.

We bought a larger house with a bigger yard so the kids would have more room. But it was an older house too. Every time we dream about remodeling, something seems to break down and use up all our remodeling money. This year it was the furnace. I guess we should try to look at the bright side: at least we don't have to spend much time haggling over what's legitimate upkeep and what's extravagant remodeling!

Oh, I know it seems terrible to complain. After all, half the world lives in mud huts or squatter's shacks and 90 percent of the world's people don't own cars.

From those statistics I hope you can tell that I do have a social conscience. Phil donates time as a tutor for the literacy council, and our deacons just asked me to help some lower-income people with their taxes. We also want to be involved in our church, so after turning down requests for years while the kids were smaller, we've agreed to team-teach Jessica's church school class.

Actually, since people view us as professionals, we're constant targets for requests for money, skill, and time.

We're glad to be able to contribute, of course. But every time we say yes, that means we have less time for each other, less time for our kids, less time for ourselves. I already know what tax season will be like. We'll just park the kids in front of the TV, subsist on fast food and convenience meals, and fall further behind in our efforts to get the kids to eat nutritiously and not be taken in by TV advertisers' lures.

"So it goes." That's what my grandma would say if she could hear me now. "Such is life, Annie." But I don't know. Sometimes I think we've got something screwed up. We wish we could figure out what God wants from us. I wish the Bible included a buyer's handbook of what you may and may not buy and a form, like the Internal Revenue Service's tax form, to determine how much to give away.

Compared to the rest of the world, we're fabulously blessed. But right now we feel financially strapped and overcommitted; we wish we were richer so life would be easier. On the other hand, we feel guilty that we have so much more than so many people do, but we don't seem to have the money or spare time to even things out.

1. What attitude does this family have toward the material blessings God has entrusted to them?

2. Using the biblical guidelines we discussed earlier as a yardstick, measure the stewardship success of this family. In what ways are they obeying God's commands? In what areas might there be need for change?

3. Anne expresses the desire for a "buyer's handbook of what you may and may not buy and a form . . . to determine how much to give away." Should the church help its members with their giving by developing such a set of guidelines—specifying, for example, whether a family may deduct the cost of Christian school tuition from their tithe? Why or why not?

Think, Pray, and Do

Think

Carefully answer the three questions asked by Ron Blue:

- Do I have enough?
- Will I ever have enough?
- Will it continue to be enough?

2. Read the parable of the rich man and Lazarus (Luke 16:19-31) and Paul's instructions to Timothy (1 Tim. 6:6-19). Try to write out for yourself a biblical, balanced theory regarding the handling of your possessions, one that you can apply to your giving and spending.

Pray

1. Read the Meditation on pages 44-45.

2. Use some of the following prayer suggestions:

   Praise: Praise God for his grace in making us his children.
   Thanks: Thank God for choosing us to be stewards of the earth's resources.
   Confession: Confess the temptation to forget the need to be continually aware of our spending and giving patterns.
   Petition: Request insight to understand better that God wants the earth's resources to be shared with all, so that no one is left hungry or cold or without clothes.
   Intercession: Pray that the gift and challenge of biblical stewardship may become an integral part of your congregation's total mission.

Do

1. Alone, or with your spouse if you are married, make a list of things you need, hope, or would like to acquire within the next three or four years. Decide whether the items fit better into "the high cost of living" or the "cost of high living."

2. Complete the following pledge as an acknowledgement that your most precious possessions belong to God.

INASMUCH as God owns everything, and

INASMUCH as I must fully accept this truth as a fact for living my life,

I HEREBY DEED THE FOLLOWING TO MY LORD AND ASSUME THEREBY THE ROLE OF STEWARD OF THESE THINGS:

1. _____

2. _____

3. _____

4. _____

5. _____

SIGNED _____

Meditation

Required: A Relationship
. . . it is required in stewards that one be found faithful.
—1 Corinthians 4:2 (ASV)

We have no choice. We are stewards. We can choose, however, what kind of stewards we will be. God requires only one thing: faithfulness. A minister once said, "We forget sometimes that God did not call us first of all to be happy; he called us first of all to be holy." Part of our holiness is faithfulness, and faithfulness rests on our relationship with our Maker.

Rigid, legalistic obedience to law is not necessarily *faithfulness.* True, in the Old Testament period, God required tithing. In the New Testament, according to Paul, God requires faithfulness. When Jesus came, humankind was redeemed and freed, so God presented this new method. The "method" can hardly be called a requirement today, because in truth stewardship is a *relationship.* The relationship is unique and is grounded in union with Christ. "For through the law I died to the law so that I might live for God. I have been crucified with Christ and I no longer live, *but Christ lives in me*" (Gal. 2:19-20). What a relationship: perfect love with imperfect gratitude, but gratitude nonetheless.

Martin Luther once said, "There are three conversions necessary: the conversion of the heart, mind, and money." To a rich young man who had conscientiously obeyed God's laws, Jesus said, "One thing you lack. Go, sell everything you have and give to the poor . . . . Then come, follow me." This young man stumbled over "his own" money, as we often do. He preferred money to the one thing he lacked, a relationship with its Owner.

God asks faithfulness of his stewards, and he places faithfulness within our reach. God gives us the ability to match his expectations. And what's more, a faithful, stewardly relationship with God greatly lessens the complexity and reduces the complications of our hurried and harried lives.

You long for simpler living? Adopt a stewardly lifestyle. God never told us to "live it up" with American consumerism. To be faithful, we need to see that we are holy, set apart by and for God. "We must realize that America is a foreign culture, as far as the life of the [Christian] is concerned," writes Terry Mattingly, communicator-in-residence on culture at Denver Conservative Baptist Seminary (*Christianity Today*, Sept. 16, '91). We need holy deviation for today's obsession with things. Our stewardly relationship with God makes this possible.

We have no choice. We are stewards, and the more we develop our relationship with God, the freer we are to be faithful stewards.

Prayer

Dear Jesus, Savior,
you are God's firstfruits.
  We thank you.
You have given us
a personal account
filled with gifts,
weeks and years,
abilities and work.
  We thank you.
Help us to see
that we cannot overdraw
our account,
because it is yours.
  We thank you.
You have asked us
to use this account
to manage your estate
on earth.
  We thank you.
We seek now
to return to you
the firstfruits
of this account—
our clock,
our work,
our education,
our checkbook.
Help us to do so
wisely,
generously,
cheerfully.
We are grateful.
Amen.

3 Managing the Master's Money

*But remember the LORD your God, for it is he who gives you the
ability to produce wealth, and so confirms his covenant, which he
swore to your forefathers, as it is today.*
—Deuteronomy 8:18

*Do not wear yourself out to get rich;
    have the wisdom to show restraint.
Cast but a glance at riches, and they are gone,
    for surely they will sprout wings
    and fly off to the sky like an eagle.*
—Proverbs 23:4-5

*Whoever loves money never has money enough;
    whoever loves wealth is never satisfied with his income.
This too is meaningless.*
—Ecclesiastes 5:10

*So when you give to the needy, do not announce it with trumpets
. . . to be honored by men . . . . But when you give to the needy,
do not let your left hand know what your right hand is doing.*
—Matthew 6:2-4

*Then Jesus said to his disciples, "I tell you the truth, it is hard for a
rich man to enter the kingdom of heaven. Again I tell you, it is
easier for a camel to go through the eye of a needle than for a rich
man to enter the kingdom of God."*
—Matthew 19:23-24

*Then [Jesus] said to them, "Watch out! Be on your guard against
all kinds of greed; a man's life does not consist in the abundance of
his possessions."*
—Luke 12:15

*For the love of money is a root of all kinds of evil. Some people,
eager for money, have wandered from the faith and pierced themselves with many griefs.*
—1 Timothy 6:10

Reflection: Forgive Us Our Debts

Steve joins a group of his friends in the fellowship room after church. "How are you, Steve?" his friend Alan says, shaking Steve's hand and smiling. "By the way, how much did you make last week?"

Steve's smile turns to wood. "None of your business," he says as cordially as possible. A few minutes later, he walks away from the group, muttering to himself about the nerve of some people. "Next thing he'll want to know is how much I spent on my new van and how much I gave to the church last year," Steve says under his breath. "He must be nuts."

Like Steve, most of us tend to think our money is our own personal business. We're secretive about how much we make and how much we give, and we tend to respect the rights of others to keep those matters secret as well. It's likely that our reasons for keeping money matters private are as varied as the people in our pews. It's also likely that at least some of us don't like to talk about how much we make because we're a little bit embarrassed about it. In a world of have-nots, we seem to be holding all the goods, and we're not quite sure what to do about it.

It may be biblical but if you ask me, that's what you get when you don't let your left hand know what your right hand is doing.

It's important to understand, first of all, that wealth, in and of itself, is not unholy; it becomes unholy only when it is misused. We need only to look at the many large gifts that both ordinary pew-sitters and wealthy Christians have contributed to the building and operation of hospitals, mission enterprises, churches, institutions, and schools to recognize that money can do a great deal of good.

But it's also true that there are many dangers in acquiring money. Wealthy persons are tempted in ways that ordinary people are not. They are tempted to place too much trust in money and its power—and even to trust money *instead* of God. They're also tempted to give themselves the credit for their riches. "Well, I worked for it!" they may think, patting themselves on the back and forgetting about their Owner, the giver of everything good.

In his review of Jacques Ellul's *Money and Power*, Robert C. Gordon says,

> Judgment falls on the person who does not recognize God's sovereignty. Ezekiel speaks against the Prince of Tyre because he credits his wealth to himself. The rich man who behaves well thinks he is righteous, yet not his conduct but the very fact that he is rich makes him, in biblical thought, unrighteous. His unrighteousness ceases only when he puts all his wealth in God's hands.

Related to Money

We all have a relationship with money. Often we don't think about that relationship when we look in our billfolds, write a check, or present a credit card. Unless we consciously have adopted a stewardly lifestyle, we tend to forget the psychological aspect of money—its ability to buy power, to win favors, to ingratiate ourselves with others, and more.

The unfortunate truth is that Christians are tempted to misuse the power of money in the same ways that other people are. Prosperity itself does not provide the Christian with purpose—it does not supply vision. Vision, rather, comes from gratitude for God's relationship with us. Through this gratitude we begin to understand that there are a variety of ways in which we can use the money that God, the Owner, has given to us. The choices we make will depend not only on how much we make and what needs our families have, but also on the way we view the world and our responsibility as God's stewards. It's essential to remember that an appropriate

49

Christian lifestyle, a lifestyle of biblical stewardship, doesn't just *happen*.

Philip Yancey, an outstanding Christian author, tells how in 1964 his high school sociology teacher forever affected Yancey's idea of wealth. The teacher said, "Do you realize that one-fourth of the people in the world earn less money in a year than I spent on the watch (worth about $50 then) I am wearing right now?" This teacher, a Southern Baptist evangelist, had done a stint in Africa in the Peace Corps. Upon his return, he had been deeply distressed by "the apathy of United States people toward a desperate world . . . . Something is wrong with a country that lets grain rot in the silos while bodies rot away in other nations" (*Christianity Today*, December 14, 1984).

Like Yancey's teacher we are often troubled by the inequity in the distribution of wealth, and wonder if there is anything we can do about it. God has not asked us to solve the problems of the world. Rather, God has called us to be open to divine guidance in our use of money, and God will show us the pathway of faithfulness.

The High Cost of Debt

An understanding of the high cost of debt and, conversely, the high return on savings, may help us in our pursuit of faithfulness. The biblical principle—we will reap what we sow—refers also to debt and savings. It's a fact: our decisions today affect our tomorrows.

Peter and Pam Ward, of Manchester, Connecticut, along with their two children Brendan, 7, and Amanda, 5, did not have a particularly merry Christmas in 1991. According to *The Wall Street Journal* (January 9, 1991), they were "haunted by the ghost of credit cards past." They are paying back a credit card debt of $40,000.

Credit cards offered freely in the mail "hooked" them both, but especially Peter. They gave themselves "cash advances," Nintendo and other expensive toys, a trip to Disneyland ($5,000), a Maine vacation, name-brand clothes, a new Ford Mustang, furs, appliances, and more.

Each day Peter dashed home to intercept the mail before Pam arrived, hoping to keep the spending alive by hiding the amount of their debt from her. But when

Peter broke his leg, laying him up temporarily, Pam started opening the mail, and the bubble broke.

Pam and Peter annually earn $60,000 between them. At this writing, they have paid $5,000 of their debt and have $35,000 to go.

Someone has said, "Today's young people want to start at the point where their parents are now." Maybe that's true. It certainly seems to have been true in the lives of Peter and Pam Ward. But we shouldn't make the mistake of glorifying the "good ol' days" and blaming all of our society's money troubles on "today" and on "today's young people."

Men and women have always coveted material possessions. Even during the Great Depression of the 1930s, there were times when Christians, like Tevye in *The Fiddler on the Roof*, raised their fist to God and asked why he couldn't spare them just a little more. People wanted (make that *coveted*) things back then too; they just weren't as tempted to buy them as we are, because they simply had no money.

Today we live in a consumer society where buying is a way of life. We are bombarded with advertising suggesting that the "good life" primarily consists of *things*. Television spends at least one-third of its time—ten minutes or more out of every thirty-minute program—showing its viewers advertisements. It shoots out commercials with the rapidity of a machine gun, and TV watchers need rock-hard willpower if they are to resist this onslaught.

Children, too, (perhaps especially) are affected. Walk down the cereal aisle of any grocery store and watch a harried mother viewing the zillions of choices she has while her children clamor for what they saw on TV. Children are programmed to consumerism in today's TV age.

What's a Christian to do in the face of such consumerism? A good place to begin is with an honest look at debt and what it does to our resources. Whenever we borrow money—to buy a house, a car, or furniture on time—we have promised that in the future we will pay that amount *plus* a stated amount for interest. We all know we pay interest on credit cards if our balance isn't paid immediately, but few of us have ever actually figured out what that credit is costing us.

And how often while making a decision about spending, saving, credit, or time payments do we pause to remind ourselves that every decision we make about spending is a *spiritual decision*? "The High Cost of Debt" (p. 54) outlines the

51

shocking expense of the debts that most of us take on quite casually.

Little did the promoters of credit, charge accounts, time payment plans, and plastic credit cards realize that their idea would turn into a monster that today is consuming its users (the total consumer debt today is competing with the national debt of around $3 trillion), breaking up marriages, and fostering bankruptcies by the thousands.

"Owe No One Anything . . ."

In view of the high cost of debt, it's not surprising that the Bible discourages borrowing. In Proverbs we read, ". . . the borrower is servant to the lender" (22:7), and the apostle Paul says, "Owe no one anything, except to love one another" (Rom. 13:8 RSV).

Yet, in spite of these warnings, it's so easy to open charge accounts or pay with plastic that the temptation to enjoy now and pay later is always with us. We need to look at the reasons for our buying. Sometimes borrowing money is necessary for our survival. But often debt reveals deeper problems: envy or greed ("keeping up with the Joneses"), lack of self-worth and self-confidence ("in order to *be* I need to *have*"), lack of self-discipline and insecurity (believing that "if I only had _____, I would feel better about myself"). We need to deal with these problems before we can follow the way of good stewards.

No matter how we disguise it, the truth is that debt can be dangerous. We simply do not know what the future holds. Currently the U.S. national debt stands near $3 trillion; the business community debt is nearly $3 trillion; and consumer debts total nearly $3 trillion. What will happen if this house of paper money falls? There isn't much we can do to stem an economic recession, but we can help ourselves by preparing to cope with it. By staying out of debt we open up our possibilities for a more stewardly future.

Planning, Steward-Style

We have seen how debt drains a large portion of our earnings. In contrast, money put into savings increases our earnings: savings beget savings.

To save, of course, we must do something that seems foreign to most in this consumer-driven society: we must spend less than we earn. It sounds so simple, yet for many of us it's very difficult. Proverbs 13:11 says it this way: "He who gathers money little by little makes it grow."

How do we begin this process? Through regularly deposited savings, no matter how small. The key is *regularity*. Savings, along with tithing and taxes, need to be deducted *first* from the paycheck. Once they are set aside, the magic of compounding can begin (see "The Rule of 72," p. 55).

Handling money—how much we choose to save, spend, borrow, or give away—is closely related to the kind of lifestyle we choose. It isn't easy to determine a lifestyle and live within it, yet as Christians we are commanded to do so.

When most of us first completed our education (whether high school, college, or graduate school), we probably looked upon our first paycheck with a sigh of relief: at last, our education had paid off! We saw so many "things" we wanted that we didn't give much thought to an appropriate lifestyle. But such a haphazard approach will not do for God's kingdom stewards. We need to review the ways in which we use our money again and again and ask ourselves, "How can I develop a stewardly lifestyle that best uses my paychecks—and any other income that I receive—as an expression of gratitude to God?"

In all our planning, it's wise to remember that tomorrow is in God's hands, and that all of our purchases, business deals, and savings deposits should be made without the presumption that "we know best" or that we have the future under control. James warns us against this kind of an attitude with these words:

> Now listen, you who say, "Today or tomorrow we will go to this or that city, spend a year there, carry on business and make money." Why, you do not even know what will happen tomorrow. What is your life? You are a mist that appears for a little while and then vanishes . . . . All such boasting is evil."
> —James 4:13-14, 16

The High Cost of Debt

Debt: Any money owed to anyone for anything.

House

The cost of borrowing to purchase a $125,000 house with a $25,000 down payment and a thirty-year mortgage:

Borrowed $100,000
Interest rate..10%
Monthly payments 877.57
Payments 30 years (360 months)....................................360

Total payments $315,925
Cost of borrowing..$215,925

Automobile

The cost of buying and financing a car, even a used car, every four years over one's working life is astonishing:

Cost of used car $10,000.00
Monthly payment @ 12½% $265.00
Total payments $12,758.40
Total cost for borrowing $2,758.40
Total cost of borrowing (interest) for the purchase of
10 cars over 40 working years $27,584.00

How to Manage Debt

Before borrowing money, ask yourself the following questions:

1. Does borrowing this money make economic sense?

2. (If you are married) Do my spouse and I agree about taking on this debt?

3. Do I have spiritual peace of mind or freedom to enter into this debt?

4. What personal goals and values am I meeting with this debt that can be met in *no* other way?

—Used with permission. Ron Blue, *Master Your Money*. Nashville: Thomas Nelson Publishers.

The Fruit of Saving

The Rule of Saving: Spend less than you earn.

The Rule of 72: 72 divided by the interest rate reveals the length of time it will take for your money to double.

To understand what that means, study the two charts on pages 55 and 56:

COMPOUNDING
TIME + MONEY + YIELD
INVESTING A LUMP SUM OF $10,000

%	5	10	15	20
2%	$11,041	$12,190	$ 13,459	$ 14,859
4%	12,167	14,802	18,009	21,911
6%	13,382	17,908	23,966	32,071
8%	14,693	21,589	31,722	46,610
10%	16,105	25,937	41,772	67,275
12%	17,623	31,058	54,736	96,463
14%	19,254	37,072	71,379	137,435
16%	21,003	44,114	92,655	194,608
18%	22,878	52,338	119,737	273,930
20%	24,883	61,917	154,070	383,376
22%	27,027	73,046	197,423	533,576
24%	29,316	85,944	251,956	738,641
25%	30,518	93,132	284,217	867,362

%	25	30	35	40
2%	$ 16,406	$ 18,114	$ 19,999	$ 22,080
4%	26,658	32,434	39,460	48,010
6%	42,919	57,435	76,861	102,857
8%	68,485	100,627	147,853	217,245
10%	108,347	174,494	281,024	452,593
12%	170,001	299,599	527,996	930,510
14%	264,619	509,502	981,002	1,888,835
16%	408,742	858,499	1,803,141	3,787,212
18%	626,686	1,433,706	3,279,973	7,503,783
20%	953,962	2,373,763	5,906,682	14,697,716
22%	1,442,101	3,897,579	10,534,018	28,470,378
24%	2,165,420	6,348,199	18,610,540	54,559,126
25%	2,646,978	8,077,936	24,651,903	75,231,638

Using current interest rates (for savings accounts, CDs, money market, etc.), answer the following questions:

1. When would your investment of $10,000 double?

2. How much would you have in ten years?

END OF YEAR VALUES

%	5	10	15	20
2%	$5,204	$10,950	$17,293	$ 24,297
4%	5,416	12,006	20,024	29,778
6%	5,637	13,181	23,276	36,786
8%	5,867	14,487	27,152	45,762
10%	6,105	15,937	31,772	57,275
12%	6,353	17,549	37,280	72,052
14%	6,610	19,337	43,842	91,025
16%	6,877	21,321	51,660	115,380
18%	7,154	23,521	60,965	146,628
20%	7,442	25,959	72,035	186,688
22%	7,740	28,657	85,192	237,989
24%	8,048	31,643	100,815	303,601
25%	8,207	33,253	109,687	342,945

%	25	30	35	40
2%	$ 32,030	$ 40,568	$ 49,994	$ 60,402
4%	41,646	56,085	73,652	95,026
6%	54,865	79,058	111,435	154,762
8%	73,106	113,283	172,317	259,057
10%	98,347	164,494	271,024	442,593
12%	133,334	241,333	431,663	767,091
14%	181,871	356,787	693,575	1,342,025
16%	249,214	530,312	1,120,713	2,360,757
18%	342,603	790,948	1,816,652	4,163,213
20%	471,981	1,181,882	2,948,341	7,343,858
22%	650,955	1,767,081	4,783,645	12,936,535
24%	898,092	2,640,916	7,750,225	22,728,803
25%	1,054,791	3,227,174	9,856,761	30,088.655

Using current interest rates (for savings accounts, CDs, money market, etc.), determine how much you would have after ten years.

Think, Pray, and Do

Think

1. In *Manage Your Money*, Ron Blue says, "Money is not only a tool, it is a test." Using examples from your own life, would you say that for you money is more often a tool than a test, or vice versa? Why? If you have a concordance and the time, you may wish to check a sampling of the Bible's references to money, and see how the Bible answers the same question.

2. Someone has said, "Don't lend anyone money unless you can consider the money a gift to that person." Evaluate that attitude.

Pray

1. Read the Meditation on page 61.

2. Use some of the following prayer suggestions:

   Praise: Praise God for his providence: he cares for us, our family and friends, church, city, state, country, continent, planet . . . the entire universe!

   Thanks: Thank God for having *chosen you*—as a person— from among the billions of people on earth.

   Confession: Confess the ease with which we spend our money with no thought that every penny of it belongs to God.

   Petition: Ask God to remove all the worries we may have concerning money and to increase our confidence that indeed he does and will care for all our needs.

   Intercession: Think of one person or family in deep distress over financial problems; ask God to show you how you may be even a small part of the answer to this prayer.

Do

1. Fill out the Balance Sheet and the Cash Flow Summary. Outline one or two steps you can take—and will take—to become a better steward over the assets God has given you.

YOUR BALANCE SHEET SUMMARY

	Before Planning	After Planning	Action Steps
ASSETS:			
Cash	$	$	
Savings			
Marketable Securities			
Life Insurance Cash Values			
Home			
Boat			
Land			
Automobile			
Furniture			
Real Estate Investments			
Other			
Other			
Total Assets	$	$	
LIABILITIES:			
Charge Cards	$	$	
Installment Loans			
Auto Loans			
Debt to Relatives			
Mortgage			
Boat Loan			
Bank Loans			
Life Insurance Loan			
Other			
Other			
Total Liabilities	$	$	
Net Worth	$	$	

58

YOUR CASH FLOW SUMMARY

	Before Planning	After Planning	Action Steps
INCOME:	$	$	
LESS:			
Giving			
Taxes			
Debt			
Total Priority Expenses	$	$	
Net Spendable Income	$_____	$_____	
LIVING EXPENSES:			
Housing	$	$	
Food			
Clothing			
Transportation			
Entertainment/Rec.			
Medical			
Insurance			
Children			
Gifts			
Miscellaneous			
Total Living Expense	$_____	$_____	
Cash Flow Margin	$_____	$_____	

—Used with permission. Ron Blue, *Master Your Money*.
Nashville: Thomas Nelson Publishers.

2. Using the Schedule of Debt and Repayment below, list all information about your debts. Note particularly the interest you will have paid if you continue to pay these debts according to the present schedule. Try to find a way, by changing something in your lifestyle, to pay more or faster.

SCHEDULE OF DEBTS AND REPAYMENT

CREDITOR	BALANCE DUE	INTEREST RATE	PAYMENT PER MO.	SCHEDULE LENGTH
1.	$	$	$	
2.				
3.				
4.				
5.				
6.				
7.				
8.				
9.				
10.				
11.				
12.				
Total	$		$	

—Used with permission. Ron Blue, *Master Your Money*. Atlanta: WTB Ministries

3. After you have taken stock of your financial situation in response to questions 1 and 2, you may want to fill in the Personal Budget Sheets (yearly and monthly) in Appendix 3a and 3b. Or photocopy these sheets and update them monthly to increase your awareness of and control over your spending.

Meditation

The S & L Crisis
Give me neither poverty nor riches.
—Proverbs 30:8

By modern definition, both John the Baptist and Jesus were poor. Both were itinerant prophets. Neither was married; neither had a family to return to each evening. John wore skins and ate locusts. Jesus wasn't sure where he would sleep each night; he probably slept under the stars more than once. Neither John nor Jesus, as far as we know, ever prayed, "Give me neither poverty nor riches."

Maybe we don't either. And we should: According to all reports, many North Americans don't know how to live in moderation between riches and poverty. Millions are in a perpetual "S & L crisis"—no savings, and a load of debt. And that's a mini-crisis compared to the horrendous savings-and-loan crisis the United States is experiencing, and for which citizens will be paying for decades!

But millions also experience another and far more serious S & L crisis, and they aren't even aware of it. Spiritual debt is far greater than monetary debt. Not everyone knows that *saving is available from Jesus Christ and that, with his blood, he marked all our debts "paid in full."* Jesus Christ is the only Way out of our spiritual "S & L crisis."

Isn't it strange, then, that Jesus also taught: "If you want to *save* your life, you will have to *lose* it. But if you want to *lose* your life, well, then, *save* it." And that's the "S & L crisis," or paradox, that you and I struggle with, isn't it?

In reality, Jesus is talking about stewardship. Treasures on earth get rusty; those stored in heaven can't be stolen or corrupted. We get that twisted sometimes. That's why the wise man said, "Give me neither poverty nor riches."

Prayer

O Lord,
we praise you
and give you thanks.
Your love endures
forever.
   Thank you.
We are so busy
with money
and things.
Yet you wait
for us to come
to you in prayer.
   Thank you.
We confess that
earthly treasure
tantalizes and
teases,
but we want
to be more holy,
with you
in the center
of our hearts.
Take your silver
and your gold.
Take our lives
and let them be,
ever,
only,
all for thee.
Amen.

4

Financial Planning: For Now and Later

This is what the LORD says: Put your house in order, because you are going to die; you will not recover.
—2 Kings 20:1

The plans of the diligent lead to profit as surely as haste leads to poverty.
—Proverbs 21:5

In the *Living Bible*, this text reads:
Steady plodding brings prosperity; hasty speculation brings poverty.

In the house of the wise are stores of choice food and oil, but a foolish man devours all he has.
—Proverbs 21:20

In the *Living Bible* this text reads:
The wise man saves for the future, but the foolish man spends whatever he has.

Four things on earth are small,
*   yet they are extremely wise.*
Ants are creatures of little strength,
*   yet they store up their food in the summer.*
—Proverbs 30:24-25

But each one should be careful how he builds. For no one can lay any foundation other than the one already laid, which is Jesus Christ. If any man builds on this foundation using gold, silver, costly stones, wood, hay or straw, his work will be shown for what it is, because the Day will bring it to light. It will be revealed with fire, and the fire will test the quality of each man's work. If what he has built survives, he will receive his reward. If it is burned up, he will suffer loss; he himself will be saved, but only as one escaping through the flames.
—1 Corinthians 3:10-15

If anyone does not provide for his relatives, and especially for his immediate family, he has denied the faith and is worse than an unbeliever.
—1 Timothy 5:8

63

Reflection: Making Life and Death Choices

Anyone who's ever switched on the T.V. or flipped through a magazine has, consciously or subconsciously, heard the message: *Spend*. It comes through loud and clear. Buy the jeans that will make you look like a new woman, the aftershave that will make you an instant social success, the cars that will turn all your friends and neighbors green with envy, the appliances that will make your work seem like play, the trip that will provide adventure and romance . . . The list goes on and on, drilling into us dozens of times each day that *luxuries* are *necessities*.

It's easy to chuckle at these ads. After all, most of them are so blatant that we can easily see through their fake promises of happiness. We really aren't so gullible that we'd be taken in by such promises, are we?

Don't be too sure. The media have far more power over most of us and the choices we make than we realize. Again and again many of us are subtly convinced that we can't do without the things that our neighbors have—so we go into debt to buy them.

Even those of us who manage to live frugally are greatly affected by our world. The planet earth may be a "foreign" culture, but it's one we're very much at home in. Sometimes it's tough to remember that Jesus said, "You do not belong to the world . . . I have chosen you out of this world."

How much is too much? What do we really need, and what can we do without? Because our understanding of "need" depends so strongly on what we get used to, those are difficult questions for Christians to answer. What one person views as a luxury is a necessity to another.

In the late sixties Watts, California, was rocked with several days of rioting. Students from a sociology class at Arizona State University were assigned to find, if possible, the causes of the rioting. All but one of the group agreed that deep-rooted poverty had caused the turmoil. (Since the students spent only a few days in Watts, and they were young and inexperienced, their analysis was too simplified, no doubt.) One young man, however, a student from Scotland, objected. He said, "All the homes I visited in Watts had both a television and a refrigerator. I don't call that poverty. At home my family has neither a TV nor a refrigerator, and we do not consider ourselves poor."

To him televisions and refrigerators were luxuries, not necessities—an idea that probably seems foreign to most of us North American consumers!

Pay Tomorrow

One of the primary factors that makes our whole consumer-crazy lifestyle possible, of course, is easy credit. We are bombarded with the idea that we needn't wait to get what we want; we deserve it now. We try hard to keep our heart fixed on our needs and on reality: God is the Owner. But, what's the harm if we have it—and, even better, if we have it *now*?

If you had $2,500 in your hands right now, would you pay off your bills? Fix up your home? Take a great vacation? $2,500 may be available for your personal use in just TWO WORKING DAYS from Transamerica Financial . . . we'll phone you to avoid delay.

So reads the junk mail from Transamerica Financial Services—and thousands of other banks and savings and loan organizations. Whether we realize it or not, advertising like that gradually nudges us toward a new way of thinking. We begin to believe we need lots of things, and we need them now.

Sometimes when we're tempted to make a purchase or take out a loan, it helps to follow the pattern of serious dieters: if the temptation to eat a brownie or a piece of apple pie ala mode is too great, the dieter walks away, postpones the eating for another day, or counts the cost. The principle is the same.

Biblical stewardship demands that we *choose* a lifestyle that will set us on course and that we stay on course through careful financial planning. Good managing of our Owner's possessions requires that we plan our expenditures wisely, hesitate to take on debt, and govern our use of money with care and prayer.

Planned Spending

Planning how we will spend our discretionary income (the amount we have left over after we pay all our bills) doesn't come easily or automatically to most people—and it's much harder for some persons than others. Yet, planning is necessary if we are to manage wisely the money "loaned" to us as an investment by the Owner.

An important part of planning is making choices, keeping in mind that the end product can be no stronger than the ingredients. Paul told the Corinthian Christians that if they built with trinkets (wood, hay, or straw) rather than with treasures (gold, silver, and costly stones), their trinkets would be destroyed with fire (1 Cor. 3:11-13). We can't fool God.

A basic part of our stewardship is the choices we make about money. Sometimes we are inconsistent in our planning. The same person who tells the church that she can't pledge a budget giving amount for the year because "I don't know whether the Lord will continue to bless me financially" signs a document at the bank, pledging to make mortgage payments for twenty or thirty years!

As we become better planners and managers, we discover that debt can become our enemy. Research and statistics show that most of North America's indebtedness reflects consumer spending for things and that when debt grows wildly (via Master Card and Visa, for example), we lose control. So as we grow in our stewardship ability, we will find it necessary to reduce or eliminate debts whenever possible.

Look at it this way—the less we tithe now the more we can give in our will, when we don't need it anymore.

Living as Kingdom Seekers

Most of us may have not chosen our lifestyle consciously. Biblical stewardship suggests that we should. A stewardly lifestyle will enhance our abilities to use well our Owner's possessions.

One thing is sure: determining our values will determine our lifestyle. Jesus said, "Seek first his kingdom and his righteousness" (Matt. 6:33). Determining values in a family requires that husband and wife talk together, pray together, and decide what is most important for their family. Do their values include yearly vacations? Christian education? Designer clothes? Music lessons for each child? New cars? Home improvements? People who are single, of course, can make their decisions alone, but it often helps to discuss choices with a Christian friend.

Income alone may never determine our lifestyle, even if we have plenty of money to live the way we wish. God's sovereignty and ownership, the gifts God has given us, the opportunities we have to develop our gifts—all are crucial elements in helping us decide how we should live.

Once a person has determined his or her lifestyle according to biblical principles, it takes diligence and vigilance to maintain it. Sometimes the purchase of one item means foregoing another. It may mean going without something or wearing the same clothes for a longer time. For some families a vacation is more important than a newer car; for many Christian families Christian education takes priority over "things." Biblical stewardship requires that we choose from among alternatives.

Do I Need a Will?

What many people don't recognize is that what we do with "our" money at death is also governed by biblical principles . . . or at least it should be. During life here on earth people accumulate wealth for many reasons, not all of which are God-approved:

1. Others advise it.

A Christian should listen to the advice of others at times, but should seek God's wisdom before acting. (Prov. 15:22; 18:15; Eph. 4:14).

2. For the envy of others.
This motive obviously is not within God's plan for Christians. (Ps. 73:2-3; Luke 12:15).

3. Because it is a game to them.
(Ps. 17:13-14; Prov. 13:11)

4. For self-esteem.
(1 Tim. 6:17; Rev. 3:17)

5. For the love of money.
This motive, too, is outside God's plan for our lives (Heb. 13:5; 1 Tim. 6:10).

6. For protection.
God shows us that we cannot protect ourselves outside of his mercy (Ps. 50:14-15).

7. Because it is their spiritual gift.
(2 Cor. 9:11; 1 Tim. 6:17-19)

Although some of these motives are obviously inappropriate and even wrong for Christians, we mustn't make the mistake of concluding that the accumulation of wealth is in itself wrong. Many people who have lived careful, stewardly lives have nevertheless gathered possessions along the way. Parents sometimes struggle financially all their lives and still find that they have accumulated some assets by the time they are senior citizens.

But although it's not wrong for Christians to accumulate things, it is mandatory that we recognize—both in life and in death—the true Owner of not only our income but also our other assets. Death is like walking away at twilight, that time of day when our shadow is longest. We may walk slowly away until we are no longer seen, but our shadow lingers. Memories of us linger in the hearts of those who love us. Memories linger, as well, in a few of the footprints we have made. They also linger in the way we choose to distribute our material goods, the possessions God has loaned us for a lifetime.

For that reason, making a will is a matter that a Christian steward will consider seriously. When we die, we won't need that car, the furniture, the house, the diamond ring, or any of those "things" we hold dear today. As someone said in jest, but with a ring of truth, "There are no U-Hauls to the cemetery."

After we die, all of our treasures will belong to others. That's a fact. And unless we make a will, the state will make our choices for us, distributing and disposing of these treasures in a fashion that often desecrates the principle that God owns everything—before and after death.

What exactly *is* a will? A will is an important legal document that contains your written *directions* for the disposition of all your owned property, as well as instructions for guardianship responsibilities where needed. A will does not, however, actually *transfer* properties or guardian rights to other persons. One way to handle the actual transfer and, possibly, to eliminate some of the inheritance or estate taxes that may occur under a will, is to make a "living trust."

A "trust" is a legal instrument that identifies who you are, describes which of your assets are affected, and sets up rules for the management of that property. A "living trust" gives the owner power over his or her assets while he or she is alive, and turns control of those assets over to another named party (without court interference) in the event that the owner becomes incompetent to manage his or her affairs or dies. Such documents are revocable; that is, they can be changed or eliminated at any point in the owner's lifetime

I dunno, I still sort of like "Firstfruits," y'know, like in Proverbs 3:9?

without any adverse effects. As you can see, the advantages of making out a living trust are numerous.

"Firstfruits" is the name not only of this course but also of the stewardship project of the Barnabas Foundation, a not-for-profit, tax-exempt charitable corporation, with headquarters in Orland Park, Illinois. The Barnabas Foundation[1] was formed in 1976 to help Christian individuals and families exercise thoughtful stewardship in a wide variety of ways by careful preparation of wills and living trusts, and tax-wise financial planning.

Parents usually leave their estate to their children, and rightly so: God requires that we care for them if we can. But leaving our children more than they need can be harmful rather than helpful. People who become wealthy through money bequeathed to them are sometimes dissolute and self-centered. So it's important to strike the appropriate balance between what we leave to our heirs and what we leave to charity. Possessions remaining at the time of our death are subject to the same principles of biblical stewardship that we follow while living.

A Child Named Charity

The Barnabas Foundation actively promotes a plan that helps people make provision for giving away some of the assets of their estates. They suggest that, when preparing a will or a living trust, people add a child named "Charity" to the will. You have two children? Well, when you add the child "Charity," your estate will be divided three ways instead of two. You have five children? Charity will become your sixth child.

It is becoming more common in estate planning to leave everything to a surviving spouse through a living trust and to make provision for the children's needs and education. A "child" called "Charity" is "born" when, in estate planning, a couple acknowledges that as grateful stewards they want to do

[1]The funding for the operation of the Barnabas Foundation comes from the more than 130 Christian charities who are members. All estate planning information and assistance is provided free and without obligation to anyone who requests it. Barnabas does not promote gifts for itself but it does encourage people to remember their own favorite Christian charities, even though some of those causes might not be Barnabas member organizations. Anyone may request a professional estate planner to personally assist him or her in preparing an estate plan that meets unique individual or family stewardship needs. This service is provided free of charge. See "Sources of Information" in session 7 for information on contacting the Barnabas Foundation.

more than simply leave everything to their children. The couple decides which charities they would like to support through their estate and, after both of their deaths, the share of their will designated for their child "Charity" is divided among those charities and ministries.

It makes sense to people to include their favorite Christian charities as a part of the "family." Such a gift reflects their belief that all that they have enjoyed on earth was a loan, a gift from the Owner, a gift that they now thankfully return to God.

Other reasons why a couple or an individual might adopt a child named Charity include the following:

a. To express thanks for help received in time of financial or spiritual need.
b. To honor a loved one who served the Lord or died at an early age.
c. To give the "large" gift that was impossible to give during their lifetimes.
d. To assure the future financial security of favorite Christian ministries.
e. To recognize that too much money, too soon, might not be good for their children.
f. To avoid extensive taxation (gifts to charity are entirely exempt from all federal and state estate taxes).

Making Lifestyle Choices

Consider three typical people with three typical lifestyles: Frugal Filmore, Middle-Class Mel, and High-Living Harry. What kind of lifestyle choices do you think each of them might make here in our own community? In what areas would you make decisions like Frugal Filmore's? Middle-Class Mel's? High Living Harry's?

	Frugal Filmore	Middle-Class Mel	High-Living Harry
Restaurants			
Clothing			
Shopping/ Stores			
Car			
House/ Neighborhood			
Vacation			
Evening Out			

Two Stories: Love It or Leave It?

Love It: Pete and Consuela Rodriguez

The name "Pete Rodriguez" means different things to different people.

- "Pete Rodriguez is a classic example of why the free enterprise system is our country's—make that our world's—best hope for survival. He's been faithful, he's been honest, he's worked hard, and God has rewarded him."

- "Pete and Consuela Rodriguez. Yes, indeed. They enjoy their wealth, and it's a pleasure to experience their hospitality. Consuela has impeccable taste in clothes, decorating, gifts and dinner parties."

- "Pete Rodriguez? Oh, yeah, the guy that got rich in the garbage business. I've heard he gives a lot of money away, but I think that anyone who moved up as fast as he did and anyone with so many contracts to manage toxic waste must have had a boost from organized crime."

- "I want to say this courteously, but I sometimes wonder if the Rodriguez family ever thinks about whether such luxurious living is justified. I happen to know that they're supporting a young couple who teach in an inner-city urban Christian school and live on almost nothing. Meanwhile, Pete and Consuela fly their four kids and I don't know how many grandkids to Hawaii or the Antilles or Europe every year for a grand reunion. That lifestyle discrepancy between the Rodriguez family and the young couple they support bothers me."

- "Not many people know this because Pete isn't one to toot his own horn, but when we were trying to raise some money for a center for handicapped children, we called on him. Without a thought or a protest, he dashed out a check for $25,000—no strings attached."

- "People say that money and power always corrupts. Pete Rodriguez is one powerful, rich guy in this area. But I was glad to have him on my side when I first came to this country. The rest of my family was still in the refugee camp. I don't know what strings he pulled, but my family's together again."

Pete himself is not at all touchy about discussing a potentially sensitive issue like wealth and its obligations.

"Some people don't relate to me as a natural peer," Pete says. "They set me apart because of my wealth. But that's kind of sad. And it seems strange to me, too, because I believe God designed all of us for accomplishment, success, and greatness.

"I also believe that it doesn't matter so much *what* you have. What matters more is *what you do with it*. My money gives me the opportunity to multiply my own witness for Christ several times by supporting others in full-time Christian ministry. I derive deep satisfaction from that.

"And I like knowing that my business provides jobs, gives people a chance to grow and develop, and helps expand the community tax base—all of which give the community the income to provide for those less fortunate.

"I hope I'm not sounding too pious and self-satisfied. Because I'm not always so sure that my view of money is the right one. On the one hand, I wonder, how can anyone see what's happening in Ethiopia and keep *anything* for themselves? On the other hand, I don't think God requires us to give everything away so we'll be poor too.

"Everybody has a different standard of living—often one that hasn't been chosen. One has certain obligations that come as a result of one's station in life. But where do you draw the line between obligation and excess? Is it O.K. to drive a Porsche, to own a yacht, to fly a private jet? I love to travel. I like this nice office. Is that self-indulgent? May I spend $10,000 for a piece of art or furniture that's aesthetically perfect?

"The Bible says that much is required from those to whom much is given. And I'll tell you, the more wealth I accumulate, the heavier the burden gets. Sometimes I wonder if I 'm capable of handling what God has given to me . . . ."

Leave It: Chuck and Virginia DeVries

When they answered a bulletin board notice in a food co-op fifteen years ago, Chuck and Virginia DeVries took the first step toward saying that, for their family, being obedient to Christ means not being upwardly mobile.

Virginia recalls, "Our starter home was almost paid off, and we were discussing whether to stay, move, or build. Although we really liked our house and many features of our neighborhood, we didn't know many Christian families nearby, and we often felt isolated. Also, a friend who worked in real estate warned us that our area was on the brink of racial change, so property values would drop. It was then that we saw a notice at the food co-op about a study and discussion group on simple living."

Chuck laughs. "We thought we'd get some leads on our dream acreage, complete with greenhouse, fruit trees, chickens, a huge garden, and a big compost pile. Actually, the group consisted of a bunch of Christians who wanted to have Bible studies and book discussions about Christian lifestyles. Even so, I remember feeling at that first meeting what I felt when I met Virginia: 'I'm home!'"

"After a few months of Bible study, I felt more like I did during our first year of marriage," Virginia comments. "I kept thinking, 'This is more than I bargained for.' I wasn't always ready to apply Christ's words on money and lifestyle personally.

"But as we all got to know each other better, sharing budgets and concerns about time and money commitments grew easier," she says. "Chuck and I decided to tithe a full 10 percent of our before-tax earnings and to give offerings on top of that. Our first two kids were already in a Christian school, so it wasn't always so simple."

Chuck says keeping to their new budget became simpler when "the neighborhood changed and house prices fell. Several of our new single and married friends moved into the neighborhood. It was like having a family of families. We started sharing freezers, tools, lawn mowers, child care . . . ."

"Sharing child care gave me the chance to get involved in the neighborhood association and a local housing ministry," Virginia says.

"As sharing freed us to tithe more, we decided to level off or reduce our standard of living despite salary increases. Again the decision was easier because it was made in community," Chuck adds.

"The reason we're all trying to live at roughly the same level is to release more money for evangelism and for development work," he continues. "If we forget our goals, we make an idol out of simple living. It's just as bad to keep *down* with the Smiths as it is to keep *up* with the Joneses. Joyful simplicity doesn't mean living without material comforts or aesthetic pleasures; it means committing yourselves to love as God's people in harmony with God's purposes for the world. It means working toward 'liberty and justice for all.'"

Virginia points to a poster of two women—one white, one Hispanic—embracing. The poster reads "A modest proposal toward peace: Let the Christians of the world agree not to kill each other."

"We talk a lot about peace and justice, about love and harmony," Virginia begins. "But I don't want to pretend that living in this city neighborhood is always easy. Whether it's legitimate or not, I feel that in an area of high population density you're a little less secure, a little more vulnerable to vandalism. And you're closer to people's pain.

"In fact, concern about single-parent families, welfare families, and just plain godless people in our area led us to some hard questions. How could we best model God's love in a way that would invite our neighbors to join in? Few of the study group members attended the same church, though many of us were Christian Reformed, Reformed, or Presbyterian. We enjoyed our get-togethers so much that some of us thought we should start a neighborhood church."

"Others of us, including me," Chuck says, "thought we should stay in our own churches. Work like yeast, you know. The public school here is terrible. I wanted a local Christian school for the families who couldn't afford it. And since we all have middle-class values— frugality, saving for the future, building durable institutions, managing our lives, conserving resources—we wanted a dozen other things here too. Like more owner-occupied homes and neighborhood businesses, a food pantry or thrift store, low-cost legal aid, health care and counseling, a better playground, more political clout . . . ."

"Lord have mercy," Virginia rolls her eyes. "It's true. If you walk around these streets, you'll see how many of our dreams the Lord turned into deeds. It's also true that on a hot, noisy summer day like today I'd rather find Jesus on some fertile island paradise where I could spend a year with Chuck, our children, our son-in-law, and our new granddaughter. I would far rather find him there than in the kids on the street, the evicted family that needs another place to stay 'for just a few days,' and all the other people in this neighborhood with so many troubles."

Talking It Over

As a Christian chooses a lifestyle, he or she must come to terms with some basic questions:

- How many luxuries can I enjoy without endangering my spiritual health?
- How many wants can I indulge in when there are so many in need?
- How much can I keep for myself and how much should I give away?
- In a world of limited resources, how many resources may I expend simply for personal pleasure?

1. How have the two couples, the Rodriguezes and the DeVrieses, answered these questions? Summarize their attitudes toward their material blessings. Then compare their attitudes toward material things with the attitudes of Naomi, Solomon, John the Baptist, and the foolish rich man in Jesus' parable.

2. What do you agree with and disagree with in the decisions of each couple? How might your answers differ from theirs?

3. What impact have the four influences listed earlier—consumerism, social setting, easy credit, and upbringing—had on each couple's lifestyle?

4. Measure each couple's decisions against Scripture. Check verses from the beginning of this chapter as well as passages from previous chapters.

Think, Pray, and Do

Think

1. North Americans enjoy "cheap food." We pay a smaller percentage of our income for food than almost any other country in the world. As a result, we often shop rather thoughtlessly. Name some concrete ways in which you can resist materialism as you grocery shop.

2. A couple took out an equity loan on their home. They invested the proceeds carefully, did not touch the capital, and used the interest to pay Christian school tuition for their children. Evaluate the parents' action in terms of biblical stewardship.

Pray

1. Read the Meditation on pages 80-81.

2. Use some of the following prayer suggestions:

   Praise: Praise God for being willing to hold us redeemed ones in loving hands, in spite of our foibles, faults, and sin.
   Thanks: Thank God for supplying all of our needs and so many of our wants.
   Confession: Confess our attachment to trinkets.
   Petition: Ask God for single-minded determination to live a life of biblical stewardship.
   Intercession: Pray for a person in need—financial or personal—whom God may lead you to assist.

Do

1. Keeping the biblical principles you discussed in the group session in mind, see if you can come up with three goals for modifying your lifestyle in the year to come.

   -

   -

   -

   Once you have set these goals, you may find that the personal budget sheets in the Appendix may help you meet them.

2. If you do not have a will or a living trust, consider talking to someone this week who can give you some advice about a will or a living trust, and who can help you create this very important document.

Meditation

Trinkets or Treasure?
If any man builds on this foundation [Jesus Christ] using gold, silver, costly stones, wood, hay, or straw, his work will be shown for what it is . . . fire will test the quality of each man's work. If what he has built survives, he will receive his reward. If it is burned up, he will suffer loss; he himself will be saved, but only as one escaping through the flames.
—1 Corinthians 3:12-15

In the nursery tale "The Three Little Pigs," the first little pig built his house of straw. The wolf blew it down. The second little pig built his of sticks. The wolf blew that one down, too. Only the third little pig used sturdy material that would last—bricks.

We're a little like the first two little pigs. Why else would Paul have to tell us to use gold, silver, and costly stones? Who wouldn't prefer them to straw, hay, and wood? It seems so simple.

But the obvious isn't always so simple. Too often we prefer the temporary trinkets of earth to the timeless treasure of heaven. Even Jesus has to remind us to "lay up for [ourselves] treasures in heaven . . . ."

One woman learned this lesson dramatically one Sunday evening. She and her husband returned from church to find that their house had been broken into. The thief had found her jewelry drawer and had scattered its contents on the floor. She looked carefully at the mass of necklaces, earrings, bracelets, and pins—her treasures. The thief had taken nothing! Her treasures were merely trinkets to the thief.

Sometimes things we "see" are more real to us because they blind our eyes to the heavenly. Elisha's servant trembled when he saw an army with horses and chariots surrounding the city. "Oh my lord, what shall we do?" he cried to Elisha. And Elisha prayed to God to "open [his servant's] eyes so he may see." God opened the servant's eyes, and he "saw the hills full of horses and chariots of fire all around Elisha" (2 Kings 6:15-17). We need to pray that our Lord will keep our eyes open to see treasure that lasts when we are blinded by trinkets that don't last.

Trinkets or treasures: a simple choice? No. The "simplicity" of the choice we make is deeply profound. It touches the essence of our lifestyle.

Treasure in heaven—eternal, infinite, forever—is possible only because of God's grace. What God makes possible he also requires. God allows and instructs us to store up treasure for the house of many rooms that our Lord is building for us in heaven (John 14:2). We build treasure in heaven when we depend on God's grace.

We are creatures of earth—smothered in trinkets. Yet our destiny is in heaven, and we may send our treasure ahead.

Amazing grace!

Prayer

Our God.
The earth is yours,
with all its fullness;
the world,
and all who live here.
    We praise you.
You see our wealth.
Sometimes we don't.
We clutch our billfolds.
We struggle.
    Lord, have mercy.
You also see the tears
    of suffering mothers;
You feel the pain
    of unemployed fathers;
You hear the wails
    of hungry babes.
Help us, Lord,
to love
as you have loved.
Forgive us, Lord, our
materialism,
consumerism, and
self-centeredness.
    Lord, have mercy.
For Jesus' sake.
Amen.

5 Communal Stewardship: Cooperation Is Essential

[Joseph said] . . . they [Egyptian commissioners] should collect all the food of these good years that are coming and store up the grain under the authority of Pharaoh, to be kept in the cities for food. This food should be held in reserve for the country, to be used during the seven years of famine that will come upon Egypt, so that the country may not be ruined by the famine.
—Genesis 41:35-36

For by the grace given me I say to every one of you: Do not think of yourself more highly than you ought, but rather think of yourself with sober judgment, in accordance with the measure of faith God has given you. Just as each of us has one body with many members, and these members do not all have the same function, so in Christ we who are many form one body, and each member belongs to all the others. We have different gifts, according to the grace given us. If a man's gift is prophesying, let him use it in proportion to his faith. If it is serving, let his serve; if it is teaching, let him teach; if it is encouraging, let him encourage; if it is contributing to the needs of others, let him give generously; if it is leadership, let him govern diligently; if it is showing mercy, let him do it cheerfully.
—Romans 12:3-8

Remember this: Whoever sows sparingly will also reap sparingly, and whoever sows generously will also reap generously . . . . And God is able to make all grace abound to you, so that in all things at all times, having all that you need, you will abound in every good work.
—2 Corinthians 9:6, 8

Do not be deceived: God cannot be mocked. A man reaps what he sows.
—Galatians 6:7

Reflection: Members of the Body

Money is a funny thing, isn't it? We're so touchy about it, and it really isn't even ours. It doesn't do us any good until we part with it. Money is a little like love; we don't have it until we give it away.

But to whom should we give it? In this fast-paced world, the media bring every inch of the globe into our living rooms, so it's impossible not to notice that our neighbors, both across the street and around the world, have needs. But how can we help them? How can we feed the starving child in Bangladesh, put a roof over the head of the woman who seeks shelter in abandoned buildings in New York City, or spread the good news in formerly communist Eastern European countries where people are starving for the gospel?

As Christians, we acknowledge that God wants us to help our neighbor. And we *want* to help. As we grow in our understanding of stewardship and try to modify our living to the style that Jesus calls us to, we want to alleviate suffering and injustice in the world around us. We want to spread the good news of Christ. But how? Where do we begin?

We can begin by admitting that the problems are too big for us to solve alone—that unless we work with other Christians, pooling our resources and abilities, our giving will not be very effective. When we approach our "neighbors" as a congregation, a denomination, or even as a group of denominations, we soon find that we are able to contribute to solutions for problems and needs that formerly seemed too big or too far away.

To make our giving more meaningful and effective, many churches and denominations have developed guidelines for giving that provide some direction for the individual family. Such systems enable the church to continue its work in a variety of different areas—to serve together through congregational and denominational ministries and agencies. Together, as the body of Christ, we demonstrate God's love.

Communal Stewardship: Congregational

Money or Ministry?

What does a system of stewardship and giving look like at the local level? Unfortunately, it is sometimes so tied in with the lists of figures and budgets that the congregation votes on each year, that members associate it more with ledgers and balance sheets than with a ministry of love.

The strong man in the circus squeezed the lemon with all his might. After a great struggle, a drop of juice finally fell out. The strong man looked out over his audience and bargained, "If anyone here can squeeze just one more drop out of this lemon, I'll pay him a hundred dollars."

One unassuming young man stepped up, took the lemon in his hands, and began to squeeze. His face strained, the blood vessels in his neck bulged, he raised his arms over his head, and—drop. One drop fell out.

The strong man said, "In all my years with the circus I have never had that happen! Tell you what I'll do. If you can squeeze another drop out of this lemon, I'll pay you five hundred dollars."

Again, the young man took the lemon and squeezed it. He squeezed and squeezed until, sure enough, another drop fell!

The strong man said to the young man, "Never in all my life has this happened. Just who in the world are you and what do you do?"

The young man said, "Oh, my name is Tom, and I'm the finance chairman down at First Church!"
—Thomas L. Are, *My Gospel of Stewardship*, pp. 65-66

We do give until it hurts. Haven't they ever heard of "low pain threshold"?

We may chuckle at this story, but it contains more than a grain of truth. Many people feel that the church is always after their money—and only their money. They view their deacons, their preacher, and their finance committee as people who are only interested in money and who try to squeeze out as much money as possible from their parishioners. They think the main purpose of stewardship is to raise money to meet the church's needs.

Of course, that's not so. God doesn't need our money. The main purpose of biblical stewardship is to raise *Christians*, not money. But it's not difficult to understand how, in our imperfect world, the church often gives the impression of being more interested in dollars than in people.

Thomas L. Are tells how a single experience changed his whole understanding of stewardship:

> Several years ago in my church we had a wealthy man named George. Every year, around Christmas, George sent the church a check for five hundred dollars. I always wrote him a glowing letter of appreciation.
>
> Then, one year, he was called on by Dr. Hazard, who was seeking a stewardship commitment from George. Halfway through his presentation, George said, "I don't need to hear your presentation. I know why you are here, and I am prepared to make a gift to the church right now. If you will wait a minute, I will write out a check."
>
> Dr. Hazard replied, "Oh, you don't understand. I am more interested in having you join us in worship than I am in picking up your check."
>
> George, unimpressed, said, "You say that, but you don't mean it. I bet you'll cash the check."
>
> Dr. Hazard took the check and, while he was speaking, tore it up, saying, "Please understand, in our church we are more interested in you and your life with us than in the money you give. Our church believes that God is more interested in our worship than our money."
>
> When Dr. Hazard related at our canvass meeting that he had actually torn up a check for five hundred dollars, some thought it was a foolish gimmick. But for the first time, I felt that I was learning something about stewardship. I wish I could tell you that on the following Sunday, George was in church, but he wasn't. His

sister telephoned to tell me how mad they were and that they had never been so insulted by the church. She said they would never come back again. To my knowledge, they never did. But although their decision still pains me, I think Dr. Hazard made one of the most authentic stewardship calls I have ever known about. He certainly did not present "God for sale" or "cheap grace."

Dr. Hazard dramatized a very important principle: *People are more important than their gifts.* What he had done felt right. I began to realize that the real issue of stewardship is not raising money.
— *My Gospel of Stewardship,* pp. 66-67

Envelopes or Free-Will Offerings?

In some congregations not only the budget itself, but also the manner of collecting it—the budget envelope—is suspect. Some folks consider the whole idea of "church envelopes" or of a "church budget" a nuisance, an unnecessary infringement on their privacy. Others believe it is legalistic, too set in its amount. It contradicts, some say, Jesus' injunction, "Let not your right hand know what your left hand is doing" (Matt. 6:3). (See comments on this point of view in chapter 2, p. 32.)

What is a "congregational budget"? It's a yearly estimate of how much the church will need to not only pay for its building costs and employee salaries, but also to conduct its ministries. For example, how much will educational materials cost for the year? How much will it take to keep the food pantry open and well-supplied? How much will you need to pay musicians and others who lead in worship? How much will it cost to send some of your young people to the summer convention or on spring ministry projects? The list can go on and on.

Just as biblical stewardship requires individual planning, so communal stewardship requires planning—both on the congregational and denominational levels.

Communal Stewardship: Denominational

Part of the money we put in that budget envelope each week—on the average, about ten dollars a family—is sent to support the work of denominational ministries and agencies. As we noted earlier, our monetary gifts are usually the only way in which we can become involved in large, faraway projects of mission, evangelism, and relief—although occasionally we also are able to volunteer or participate in some hands-on way in the work of one of these agencies.

The Christian Reformed World Relief Committee (CRWRC) is an outstanding example of an organization that uses both volunteers and cash contributions to make its ministry possible. (CRWRC is supported by voluntary contributions only; it is not included in the quota for denominational ministries of the Christian Reformed Church.)

During the 1990-91 fiscal year CRWRC disbursed to:

Bangladesh.........1000 tons of wheat for cyclone victims
El Salvador ....600 tons of corn, beans, flour, and milk powder for war refugees
Ethiopia ....1000 tons of wheat for drought victims
Liberia ....160 tons of beans/oil for child-feeding programs
Sudan ....1350 tons of wheat/corn for drought and war victims.

The cost of the above exceeded $1.5 million!

In addition, more than two hundred and fifty CRWRC volunteers repaired nearly three hundred homes for poverty-stricken and elderly people living in the area of South Carolina that was battered by Hurricane Hugo. Executive Director John DeHaan wrote in his director's report,

Are there any benefits to keeping our eyes sternly focused on results? Just listen to this—your dollars are used to help people to become self-sufficient in Jesus' name and in the most stewardly manner possible. For example, approximately ten years ago it cost CRWRC over $500 per family, each year, to move them toward self-sufficiency, and a little over 13,000 families were being served. Last year, we served 71,145 families (overseas) at a cost of slightly more than $144 per family, which now *includes* administrative and public relations costs.

Giving with Confidence

Why give to CRWRC and our many denominational boards and agencies, when so many other causes are pleading for our dollars as well? The best place to be confident that one's gifts are being used in a stewardly manner is in one's denomination. Here each agency or ministry budget is scrutinized with care and with an eye focused on accountability. Each agency must submit to a "watchdog" committee of the denomination a well-documented financial annual budget before its request may be submitted to the annual synod, the ruling body that will decide the amounts each agency will receive (see 1991-92 budget in Appendix 5a).

Unless a church is "non-denominational" or "independent," it usually is part of a denomination—an association or federation of churches that have the same kind of church government or confess the same doctrines. The denomination as such has many tasks or ministries that exceed the ability of what churches are able to do individually. Supporting missionaries, for example, requires more money than one average church can raise by itself (in addition to its congregational needs). When each church pays a share, however, much can be accomplished.

Several families living in Burke, Virginia, in the late sixties worshiped in a Christian Reformed Church in Washington, D.C. They were accustomed to worshiping twice on Sunday, but the distance to Washington required quite a bit of time and travel for them each Sunday.

They began to meet as a North Virginia household group on Sunday evenings. Before long they decided to meet each Sunday morning as well. They asked chaplains, of whom there were many on the east coast, to conduct their services.

The group of families soon decided that they wanted to be an organized church. But because they didn't have enough money to start a new church on their own, they contacted the Home Missions ministry of the Christian Reformed Church. After consultation, necessary field work, and a survey of the area, Home Missions agreed to help them. The agency asked Rev. William Ribbens to become the congregation's first pastor, agreeing to pay his salary and provide him with a home.

When Rev. Ribbens left in 1971, Rev. Verne Guerkink became the small congregation's new pastor. At that time Home Missions made an agreement with the church, promising to continue to help the congregation on an annually declining basis—so that by the end of the tenth year of its existence, the congregation would be independent and self-sufficient. And that's what happened. Today they are a self-supporting congregation of about fifty families, many of whom work for the government.

According to Jack De Vos, Home Missions' director of development and communications, during the ten years the Burke, Virginia, church was assisted by Home Missions, it received nearly $225,000—money gathered through the quota system from *all* the churches in the Christian Reformed denomination. Without this help, the initially small group of ten to twelve families could not have survived and developed.

How much did it cost families in the CRC to help this new church in Virginia develop and grow? Based on a denomination of 300,000 persons, the amount contributed by each person over the ten-year period was only 75 cents. That's only seven and a half cents per person per year!

Sometimes the amount the denomination asks of each family per year seems like a lot. But when you take a careful look at all of the ministries that your money supports and all of the smaller projects (such as the Virginia church) that each of those agencies is able to begin or support, that amount begins to seem like a glorious opportunity instead of a burden!

With these gifts from each member of the denomination, the Christian Reformed Church is able to support many missionaries, both at home and abroad, and to provide Christian literature in seven languages. The denomination has its own radio and television ministry and supports a college and seminary. It subsidizes many chaplains who serve in the armed services or in hospitals, and it provides funds for committees that help the mentally and physically disabled. The church also provides educational materials and a denominational weekly magazine, both of which generally support themselves.

The usual procedure for determining the amount needed each year by the denomination is as follows:

1. Each ministry or agency carefully prepares its budget for the coming year. The budget is based on monies needed for missionaries or others involved in the ministry itself: actual expenses (rent, utilities, etc.), administration (salaries, office expenses, travel), and other expenses.
2. Each ministry submits this proposed budget to the denominational treasurer and a financial committee. This com-

mittee, in cooperation with the requesting ministry, reviews the budget and decides whether the total amount of the budget should be raised, lowered, or submitted to the synod as requested.

3. The accepted budget is submitted to the annual synod (the governing body of the church), where it is assigned to a "financial affairs committee." All the requested budgets are again reviewed carefully, and members of the agencies are permitted to explain the details of their needs. The amounts are agreed upon by this financial affairs committee.

4. The synod, a body currently (1990) consisting of 168 members who also have reviewed the agency and ministry budgets, accepts or rejects the budgets. (Because the preliminary review has been done so carefully, budgets are seldom changed at this level.)

5. The various amounts of the individual ministries and agencies are totalled, and this amount is divided by the number of families in the denomination. This final amount is called *quota,* a word that unfortunately fails to emphasize the opportunity this communal giving affords each member of the denomination.

6. Each congregation in the denomination decides how it counts its families and is asked to pay an appropriate amount.

(You'll find a breakdown of the 1991 "quota" or ministry needs of the Christian Reformed Church in Appendix 5a, along with a list of other agencies and causes recommended to the church for support through special offerings.)

Sometimes members feel that the quota is more like a tax than a contribution. But that's not so. Perhaps to clarify what the system is and does, the phrase *ministry share* should replace the term *quota.* The quota is the individual *share* each member pays for denominational ministries and for administration. A deeper understanding of biblical stewardship will help us appreciate quota as *opportunity*—an opportunity we are given to be able to serve in many ministries.

The Lord Needs It

The prophet Malachi (3:6-12) summarizes well what God admonishes, challenges, and promises:

"I the LORD do not change. So you, O descendants of Jacob, are not destroyed. Ever since the time of your forefathers you have turned away from my decrees and have not kept them. Return to me, and I will return to you," says the LORD Almighty.

"But you ask, 'How are we to return?'

"Will a man rob God? Yet you rob me.

"But you ask, 'How do we rob you?'

"In tithes and offerings. You are under a curse—the whole nation of you—because you are robbing me. Bring the whole tithe into the storehouse, that there may be food in my house. Test me in this," says the LORD Almighty, "and see if I will not throw open the floodgates of heaven and pour out so much blessing that you will not have room enough for it. I will prevent pests from devouring your crops, and the vines in your field will not cast their fruit," says the LORD Almighty. "Then all the nations will call you blessed, for yours will be a delightful land," says the LORD Almighty.

That text is as true today as the day it was written. When that day comes that we "test the Lord," and our church's income can serve congregational and denominational needs far beyond the budgets, then our communal biblical steward-

After five months of paperwork, loans, title companies, and closings, I thought we had ownership pretty well defined.

ship will be in full bloom. Returning to God what is his is indeed a spiritual experience.

Sometimes, though, we "grow weary in well-doing." Dr. Dennis Hoekstra, in one of his inimitable "stewardship talks," told a story.

> There is a little story within a story in the Luke 19 account of Jesus' triumphal entry that has been both helpful and surprising to me (Luke 19:28-40).
>
> Among other things, according to this passage, Jesus' initiation of worldwide kingship required two things. One, he needed dedicated followers who dared to make bold requests: Give me your donkey! Why? Simply because "Our Lord needs it." Two, he needed a willing giver.
>
> Obviously both the asker and giver were blessed, and Jesus' work moved forward, according to this story, only because someone dared. In fact, the Lord himself commanded that the person ask boldly for the material resources needed to further Jesus' *worldwide* redemptive work.
>
> Lest we become too self-important, self-righteous, or manipulative in this task, Jesus assures us in verse 40 that if we as askers and givers falter or fail, he will take over. Since he does in fact own and control all the material resources we so glibly claim to own, even the stones themselves can be used to accomplish his world-renewing ministry. But then, as now, he chooses to use both bold askers and willing givers to accomplish his work in the world.
>
> So the next time we grow weary or are put down by the notion that our work is mostly bothersome and is sometimes suspected as money grubbing, remember these words, *"The Lord needs it."*

Bible Study: Communal Giving

To the Local Congregation

Read Acts 2:44-47 and 4:32-35.

Although, as we noted in chapter 1, the simple "common sharing" of the early Christians is probably not possible in our complex society, some of the basic principles of giving that these men and women lived by are an excellent model for giving for all congregations. Think about each of the following descriptions or principles. How well does each one apply to your congregation? What concrete changes could you make in your ministry to make these statements more of a reality in your congregational living?

1. All the believers were one in heart and mind.
2. There was not a needy person among them.
3. No one claimed that any of his or her possessions was his or her own.

To the Larger Church and Beyond

Read 2 Corinthians 8:1-15.

In this passage, Paul talks to the Corinthians Christians about giving money for the needy Christians in Jerusalem. He holds up the Macedonian churches as a model of Christian giving.

1. How does Paul describe the giving of the Macedonian Christians, a giving motivated by God's grace? In particular, what does it mean to "give as much as [you are] able, and even beyond [your] ability"? What effect might looking to the Macedonians as a model have on giving in your denomination?

2. Paul stresses the importance of equality in the church. He says, "At the present time your plenty will supply what they need, so that in turn their plenty will supply what you need." Use some concrete, contemporary examples to show the meaning of those words for our giving today.

Case Study

For the deacons of an average sized (100 families) Christian Reformed Church in the midwest, preparing the annual budget for the following year is a four-month process.

September

The deacons review the receipts for the first eight months of the year and note that offerings and budget envelopes are not providing the amount they need to meet all the expenses of the current year.

One deacon says, "The preacher should preach a good, stiff sermon on giving; *then* they would give." Not all deacons agree. After some discussion, the deacons decide to (1) advise the congregation of the shortage, (2) urge members to contribute who may have forgotten during summer vacations, and (3) ask committee heads and program directors to spend cautiously, and, if possible, to project their needs for the following year.

October

The deacons are encouraged by the response of the congregation and find that receipts almost equal expenditures. Estimates of needs for the next year are in; only one remains to be submitted.

The ministry staff has requested that $2,000 be added to the budget to pay for a food-and-clothing ministry. What should the deacons do? Some feel that the minister's raise and inflationary increases in almost all other expenses make it impossible to add another $2,000 to the budget. They suggest that the deacons instead ask the congregation for separate contributions for the food-and-clothing ministry. To help focus the discussion, one deacon places several headings on the chalkboard.

Worship expenses	$1700.00
Education	2825.00
Fellowship and Caring	200.00
Administrative expenses	58988.00
Building, maintenance	24292.00
Building fund	8000.00
Denominational ministries	38770.00
Total	$134775.00

Some deacons feel a food-and-clothing ministry is much needed and is a ministry that should be supported by the entire church. After all, the church has an obligation to the community and "fellowship and caring" currently receives just a token amount in the budget. But another deacon points out that the "denominational ministries," the second largest item of the budget, have "caring" as their focus.

After further discussion, the deacons decide to table the request until November when they will invite the minister and ministry staff to meet with them.

November

The minister and the ministry staff meet with the deacons. They discuss the proposed ministry at length and spend some time in prayer. They agree that the minister will mention the ministry "in an appropriate fashion" from the pulpit, that it will be announced in the bulletin, and that the ministry staff will write an article about it in the church newsletter.

In addition, the deacons will take a step that has never before been taken in their church: they will ask the congregation for faith-promise pledges before setting the budget for the following year. The minister will include information on the faith-promise pledge in his presentation of the need.

The deacons hand out or mail to all members of the congregation the form for faith-promise pledges. Almost the entire congregation responds.

December

The deacons add up the amounts of the faith-promise pledges . . . .

1. Write your own ending to the case study. As you do, keep some of the following questions in mind. Was the faith-promise pledge appropriate in the situation? Would people be more likely to give more under the faith-promise system than they would have normally? Is it appropriate for deacons to ask for pledges, or should offerings be personal?

2. Does a church operate on a budget in a way that is similar to a family budget? Which way, do you think, would be a better way for a church to prepare its annual budget: (1) determine how much the church "needs" and divide it by the number of families in the congregation, expecting each family to pay the same amount, (2) determine how much the church needs and prorate it among the number of individuals and/or families according to their ability to pay, or (3) ask the members of the congregation to make faith-promise pledges for the coming fiscal year and then prepare a budget based on those commitments?

3. Compare the problems faced by the deacons in the story to those faced by your congregation. How does your congregation organize its giving? In what way might the system be improved?

Think, Pray, and Do

Think

1. Read sections 44-58, "The Mission of God's People," from the Contemporary Testimony *Our World Belongs to God* (see *Psalter Hymnal*, pp. 1033-1038). In thinking about the "mission of God's people," consider how many and which ministries you can do better as an individual than as a member of a church or community of believers. What do you conclude?

2. The government is constitutionally required to promote the general welfare of the people. How effective today is the individual Christian citizen in promoting God's goodness through government? Think about some things *groups* of Christians are doing. Could Christians be more effective in communal stewardship of the Master's money if they would combine their resources and power as a Christian political party? Why or why not?

Pray

1. Read the Meditation on pages 99-101.

2. Use some of the following prayer suggestions:

   Praise: Praise God for promising to come again to bring us home.

   Thanks: Thank God for the Holy Spirit who, by his power, constantly gives us hope, joy and peace.

   Confession: Confess our frequent failure to live as people "in transit," people traveling from the planet Earth to that new homeland Christ is preparing for us (John 14:1-4).

   Petition: Ask God for holy energy to communally as well as individually demonstrate to the needy and the hurting the love and compassion of our Savior.

   Intercession: Pray for the missionaries, workers, and volunteers who are "on the front lines" while we on the home front supply the necessary equipment and dollars.

Do

This week choose someone involved in missions to pray for daily: a pastor, nurse, doctor, teacher, social worker, agricultural expert, or a child of such workers. Pray for that person daily. Write to him or her regularly. Find ways (other than the financial support you already provide) to encourage that person. Assure him or her that as Christians we work together and that distance does not separate us in our efforts to be stewards for our Master. If your church does not support a person whom you can particularly befriend, request a name from one of your denominational ministries.

Meditation

Hope

"The Lord himself will come down from heaven . . . and the dead in Christ will rise first. After that, we who are . . . left will be caught up together with them in the clouds to meet the Lord in the air. And so we will be with the Lord forever.
—1 Thessalonians 4:16-17

The old man was visiting his children and grandchildren. As he left the family room to retire, his four-year-old granddaughter said, "Good night, Gramps. See you in the morning."

"Yes, honey, I hope so. Goodnight," Grandpa replied, and kissed her on the cheek.

"Why does Grandpa say, 'I hope so'? Doesn't he want to go to heaven?" Nancy asked her father.

"Of course he does, honey," said Dad, "but he also knows that if he dies tonight, he won't see us anymore . . . at least until we all get to heaven. He knows he would miss us."

Although his answer satisfied Nancy, Dad continued to puzzle over it. The paradox of the love of life and the longing for heaven remained with him into the night . . . .

What is *hope*? Webster's Ninth New Collegiate Dictionary defines it in this way: "to cherish a desire with expectation of fulfillment" (p. 581). Then, in apparent contradiction, the dictionary adds that "trust" is an archaic meaning of the word *hope*. How can that be? Maybe Grandpa used the word more correctly th an he realized. He *cherished* the idea of another day with his family, but he didn't believe (*trust*) that it would necessarily be so.

We *hope* for lots of things: sunshine for the picnic; a promotion on the job; that the children do well in school; and more. And sometimes we lose hope. Any person (especially a Christian) who has been sucked and swooshed downward in the powerful vortex of depression knows the malignancy of hopelessness. Absolute hopelessness is a frozen bottomlessness, an excruciating sickness of the spirit. There is no hope because there is no trust, and vice versa.

Hope without trust is hollow. A wish at best. We Christians know a hope that is based on trust.

But there are times when we grow weary: bone-weary. Yes, we are willing and grateful managers of the Master's money, but with the French priest, Michel Quoist (*Prayers*, New York: Sheed and Ward, 1961, pp. 118-119), we sometimes cry:

> The first came in, Lord. There was, after all, a bit of space in my heart.
>
> I welcomed them. I would have cared for them and fondled them, my very own little lambs, my little flock.
>
> You would have been pleased, Lord; I would have served and honored you in a proper, respectable way.
>
> Until then, it was sensible. . . .
>
> But the next ones, Lord, the other men—I had not seen them: they were hidden behind the first ones.
>
> There were more of them. They were wretched; they overpowered me without warning.
>
> We had to crowd in, I had to find room for them.
>
> Now they have come from all over in successive waves, pushing one another, jostling one another.
>
> They have come from all over town, from all parts of the country, of the world; numberless, inexhaustible.
>
> They don't come alone any longer but in groups, bound one to another.

They come bending under heavy loads; loads of
injustice, of resentment and hate, of suffering and
sin . . .
They drag the world behind them, with every-
thing rusted, twisted, badly adjusted.
Lord, they hurt me! They are in the way, they are
all over.
They are too hungry: they are consuming me!
I can't do anything any more; as they come in,
they push the door, and the door opens wider . . .
Ah, Lord! My door is wide open!
I can't stand it any more! It's too much! It's no
kind of a life!
What about my job?
My family?
My peace?
My liberty?
And me?
Ah, Lord! I have lost everything: I don't belong
to myself any longer;
There's no more room for me at home.
"Don't worry," God says, "you have gained all."
"While men came in to you,
I, your Father,
I, your God,
Slipped in among them."

Yes, when we grow tired, God slips in. He speaks *hope*
to us. He whispers, "I am coming again to bring you to me.
I have told my prophet Isaiah (40:31), 'those who *hope* in
[Me] will renew their strength. They will soar on wings
like eagles; they will run and not grow weary, they will
walk and not be faint.'" What a marvelous hope we have!

The four gospel accounts are a magnificent, holy arrow
pointing to the cross and to the resurrection. . . . the
bedrock of our hope. And with hope our lives as grateful
biblical stewards fall again into place. Pilgrims travel in the
hope of heaven tomorrow. We go forward, managing glad-
ly our Master's money, individually and communally.

"May the God of hope fill you with all joy and peace as
you *trust* in him, so that you may *overflow* with hope by the
power of the Holy Spirit" (Rom. 15:13). And one day,
some day, we will be with our Lord forever.

Prayer

Father, Son,
and Holy Spirit—
We praise you
as One in three
and three in One.
For creation,
salvation,
and resurrection,
    we thank you.
For opportunities,
gifts,
and money,
    we thank you.
For selfishness,
stinginess,
complacency,
    forgive us, we pray.
In Jesus' name,
Amen.

6

Teaching Stewardship

Only be careful, and watch yourselves closely so that you do not forget the things your eyes have seen or let them slip from your heart as long as you live. Teach them to your children and to their children after them.

—Deuteronomy 4:9

Impress them [the commandments] on your children. Talk about them when you sit at home and when you walk along the road, when you lie down and when you get up. Tie them as symbols on your hands and bind them on your foreheads. Write them on the doorframes of your houses and on your gates.

—Deuteronomy 6:7-8 (repeated in Deut. 11:18-20)

Train a child in the way he [or she] should go,
  and when he [or she] is old he [or she] will not turn from it.

—Proverbs 22:6

If anyone does not provide for his relatives, and especially for his immediate family, he has denied the faith and is worse than an unbeliever.

—1 Timothy 5:8

If anyone has material possessions and sees his brother in need but has no pity on him, how can the love of God be in him? Dear children, let us not love with words or tongue but with actions and in truth.

—1 John 3:17-18

Reflection: By Word and Deed

Twenty-year-old Jeff, a college sophomore, had just bought his first car. It was a sporty, six-year-old Ford, bright red, with 100,000+ miles. Although it was in near-show-car condition on the outside, it was dilapidated mechanically. "Coulda' done much better for $700 less," complained Grandpa, who financed the purchase interest-free, "but no, he has to have one of those sporty jobs." Jeff just smiled at his grandpa and went on his way.

As time went by, Jeff grew more and more pleased with his purchase. Although his parents, grandparents, and friends warned him that his car was an "in-the-city-only" model, Jeff knew otherwise. After all, *he* was the one driving the car. He had been driving it for weeks to work and school with no problems. Why did people get so worked up over something as trivial as high mileage?

So when Jeff's friends invited him to come for a weekend visit at their college, Jeff eagerly accepted. A few hours on the road sounded like the break he needed, and you couldn't really call three hundred miles a *long* trip, could you? He was pretty certain that even Grandpa wouldn't object. Besides, he was on his own now, and it was time he made his own decisions . . . .

At least until the car broke down about two hundred miles from home.

Standing at the side of his lifeless car in the pouring rain, Jeff didn't feel quite as confident as he had when he began his trip. So when the wrecker brought him and his car to a service center, Jeff called his dad. "I need some money, Dad," Jeff explained. "The mechanic says I need a new alternator, and the sales guy here says it will cost $120.00. I've only got $15.00 with me."

Jeff, like thousands of other children, young people, and, yes, even adults in our culture, has a lot to learn about managing money. He's fallen into the trap that lures so many in our society—the glitzy exterior—and he's looking for someone to bail him out—as usual. How his father responds to his cry for help will determine, to some degree, what types of choices Jeff will make about purchases and accepting responsibility in the future.

That puts Jeff's Dad in a tough position—one many of us often find ourselves in as well. What response will do the most to *teach* this young man about value, responsibility, and stewardship?

Challenged to Teach

We cannot escape teaching. We *are* teachers, all of us. We teach most of the time that we are awake. Children and young people learn from us—whether the learning is intentional or not. They also learn from the rest of the culture that surrounds them. What many people don't realize is that much, maybe most, of life's basic learning is *caught* rather than *taught*.

From what or whom are our children learning? By the time they are eighteen years old, children have spent as much time in front of the television as in the schoolroom. Scary, isn't it? In the face of such statistics, the challenge to parents is tremendous. The rot and garbage of much (not all, by any means) of today's media need to be supplanted with the love of Jesus Christ. This comes as no small order—but we are asked only to plant. The season for planting is as long as life.

The challenge to the church—the body of Christ—is also great. Whenever a child is baptized, we as a congregation promise to help the parents rear their children in the Lord. (If we were to ask ourselves how many times we have made this promise in the past year, we probably couldn't even remember!)

God instructed the Israelites (Deut. 4:9) about their duty as teachers in considerable detail. He warned them not to allow their growing affluence to blind them to the truth that all that they "owned" belonged to God:

> Only be careful, and watch yourselves closely so that you do not forget the things your eyes have seen or let them slip from your heart as long as you live. Teach them to your children and to their children after them.

And in Deuteronomy 11:19-20:

> Teach them to your children, talking about them when you sit at home and when you walk along the road, when you lie down and when you get up. Write them on the door frames of your houses and on your gates . . . .

Proverbs 22:6 contains both a command and a promise:

Train a child in the way he [or she] should go,
and when he [or she] is old he [or she] will not turn
from it.

The word *train* comes from an Arabic word meaning "to create a pucker." In order to stimulate a newborn's suck, Arabic midwives would crush dates and apply the mixture to the child's palate. The child would put his tongue up to the roof of his mouth and begin a sucking action. *Training*, then, literally means to create a pucker, a hunger in the child as to the way he should go (taken from *Crown Ministries, Small Group Financial Study*, ch. 10).

The more we teach our children during all their growing-up years, both by word and by example, the more deeply ingrained an idea will become. A young woman who had strayed through the evil labyrinth of alcohol, drugs, prostitution, and infidelity, told her friends upon her conversion, "The roots my mother planted were just too deep. I couldn't tear them out no matter how hard I tried. The 'Hound of Heaven' finally caught me."

A Way of Life

Financial responsibility is certainly one thing God expects parents to teach their children. In a culture as dominated by materialism as this one, that is no easy task. As our children move toward adulthood, they often expect to go on living at the same level of comfort and affluence they became accustomed to while living with their parents. Because their parents haven't adequately taught them the realities of money and money management, they make the mistake of assuming they will "start out" at that point where their parents are now: a mortgage-free house, one or even two cars in the garage, and an annual vacation certainly look good.

Parents who witness the financial difficulties of an older child and in compassion give or loan money to that child must realize that this gift or loan changes the relationship between them and their child. The old saying "who holds the purse holds the power" contains much truth. While it's true that Timothy (1 Tim. 5:8) teaches that we must take care of our relatives, his advice does not include the word *always* or the phrase "whenever he or she needs money." The idea that "my parents will take care of that," or, "let's ask Dad; he's always good for a loan," is born in childhood. The attitude toward money that Jeff had at age twenty had roots in Jeff's childhood.

The bottom line is that there are no Band-aids. There are no quick cures for lessons poorly taught in childhood. The best way for parents to teach children to become financially responsible is through a consecrated lifestyle that vibrates with awareness of stewardship. If biblical stewardship is our lifestyle, it is also part of us, and it will be evident. It's something we will be teaching at the dinner table; while telling bedtime stories; on birthdays; in the stores while shopping with the children; during discussions about children's wants ("everybody has one; I'll be the only one without"); and in church, especially when special offerings are requested.

Probably the most important thing we can teach our children about biblical stewardship is that it is a *lifestyle*—a way of life that continues until death and that even at death is reflected in the disposal of our earthly goods. It affects giving, saving, borrowing, purchasing, planning, working, and playing.

Living the stewardly lifestyle in today's culture, as we know, is anything but easy. Still, we have new life in Jesus Christ, a life we now live by faith in Jesus Christ. In that freedom and in that strength, we have abundant power . . . and our heavenly "bank" has compounded interest far greater than any earthly bank. That's what our children must experience early in life.

Tips for "Teachers"

Admitting the importance of equipping our children to be good stewards is an important step. But what's the best way to go about it? Is it enough to hope that children will learn from our example—that nothing needs to be said or done?

Probably not. It's important to keep in mind the different ways in which children learn. They learn not only from what they see us do but also from what they hear us say—and perhaps especially through what *they do* themselves. For example, children will best learn how to give generously if (1) they see us giving generously, (2) we tell them about the importance of generous giving, and (3) they have opportunities to give generously themselves—and are praised for it.

What We Do

I'd rather see a sermon than hear one any day.
I'd rather you work with me than merely point the way.
The eye is a more ready pupil than ever was the ear.
Good advice is often confusing, but example is always
clear.

This anonymous verse says it well. Most, if not all, of our words are useless unless we practice what we preach. We can talk about the importance of giving generously, but if our children see us reluctantly pull out a dollar bill or two for the special offering, if they hear us grumbling about the church budget, if they see us giving stingily, they will be far more impressed by our example than by our words.

On the other hand, if they see us giving "till it hurts," with smiles on our faces; if they notice how eagerly we pledge help to the family in the neighborhood who lost everything in a fire; if they sense the importance we place on offerings and the thought and prayer that lie behind our giving—those examples too will have an impact on their own style of living and giving.

What They Do

Perhaps the most powerful kind of learning is experience. Instead of just watching their parents and taking note of what their peers are doing, children must become *involved* in stewardship. Through doing, through experiencing what it feels like to give, they will learn more than they might through anything their parents might show or tell them.

We can design practical situations in which our children can practice stewardship quite naturally. Some of the following ideas may work well for you and may inspire you to think of others that are uniquely appropriate for a specific child or situation.

1. *They're mine.* Young children seem instinctively possessive about their toys. "They're mine," a two-year-old will cry and grab for everything in sight. Sharing can be initiated early and gently, and it is an important part of stewardship.

2. *I'm full.* At first glance one doesn't think of dinner as a time to teach stewardship, but it can be. Older folks will remember depression years when "clean your plate," "turn

off the lights," and "close the door—you're wasting heat"
were commands made to save money. Stewardly suggestions, yes, but they sprang from desperate need and weren't
exactly the acts of gratitude that biblical stewardship
requires.

The idea that waste is not good stewardship still needs
to be taught, however. What North America is wasting
today while millions cry to heaven for food, clothing, shelter, and work is a challenge we must cope with. Teaching
children to choose small portions—only as much as they
can eat—is a small beginning. Children who are too young
to gauge how much they can eat need parental help in
determining the size of their portions.

3. *It's MY allowance.* Some parents give their children
   allowances—an appropriate context in which to teach
   both tithing and budgeting and the importance of giving
   to the Lord *first.* "Do I have to give 10 percent?" is a question most parents who have attempted this practice have
   encountered. Because children may not have matured
   enough spiritually to *want* to give, parents may have to
   kindly insist on a tithe. Remember stewardship is of grace;
   it is not determined by law but by our relationship with
   our Father.

4. *That's not my job.* If you believe children should not be
   paid for chores, but that chores are a legitimate and
   healthy sharing of the work that comes with living as a
   family, you can use this idea to explain stewardship in
   terms of caring for one another. Children, within their
   own limits, can carry out their stewardly responsibilities by
   sharing in the work that makes a house a home.

5. *So much for that.* Teach the children simple budgeting.
   Perhaps you hate budgets, and you're not good at keeping
   them. If this series of lessons has encouraged you to develop a budget so that you can plan your purchases more
   wisely, it may be a good time to try it *together with the children.* Envelopes for giving, saving, clothing, and spending
   money may provide a simple way to begin.

6. *Together we can do it.* Plan a giving project with the children. Determine what share each one will pay and how
   long the project will take. Through this you can demonstrate not only planning, but proportionate giving as well.

7. *I'd rather have a . . .* In midsummer, have each child estimate a list of clothing he or she will need when school begins again. Discuss the list as carefully and as objectively as possible. Estimate the costs. Set priorities (if you get this, you can't get that, and so forth). Then determine how the clothing will be paid for and suggest that the child may wish to buy one or two of the pieces herself or himself. This will help the child learn to plan and make choices.

8. *Let me put something in.* Have each child deposit his or her own gift in the offering plate on Sunday. Some congregations have two offerings, one for the church budget and one for special causes. Share with the children what a church "budget" is, and explain why the family puts either a check or cash in an *envelope* rather than directly into the offering plate.

   If your church bulletin announces the special offering a week in advance, take time (Sunday dinner may be a good opportunity) to discuss the purpose of the offering and to encourage the children to think about what they might like to give. It is important for children to see how extensive the work of the kingdom of God is here on earth and how we may communally support it.

9. *I want it now.* Grownups have a hard time waiting for the things that they want. Think how much harder it must be for children! When one of your children wants a big item, discuss it carefully with him or her. Consider setting a timetable: ask the child to contribute a certain amount for the item each day or week, and promise to contribute a certain amount yourself. Talk about how long it will be until you've saved enough to purchase the item.

   If the child is very young, the waiting time should be very short. Older children can wait longer, but it helps to chart the progress they are making so that they can keep their eye on the goal. Some parents prefer to wait until the child's portion is completely paid before contributing. Others make regular installments with their child. This activity will help teach delayed gratification, an idea that is so necessary in learning to control one's credit expenses later in life.

10. *My own account.* Open a savings account for or with your child. Even though the deposits may be small, the account

will provide a visible way for the child to learn about interest, perhaps even compound interest. Encourage the children to save at least part of cash gifts they may receive for birthdays, Christmas, or other occasions.

What We Say

Although the most dramatic learning probably occurs in response to "doing" or watching what others are doing, words also have their place in teaching. When teaching children, some truths need the kind of explanation that only words can provide. It's up to you to decide when it will be most meaningful to discuss giving, to explain why we give, and to explain for what and for whom we give the money we've been given.

The following suggestions may be helpful for you. Many of them take the form of devotions and may be incorporated into your family worship around the table.

1. *Read Psalm 24.* This psalm speaks of God as the Owner of all and the King of glory. In other words, God isn't just a wealthy person; he is king of everything and everyone. As a family, talk about the meaning of the word *all*—in the lives of Dad and Mom and in the lives of each child. A mother and a daughter were discussing the meaning of the word "all," and the conversation went like this:

   > "Do you mean God owns my sand box?" "Yes." "Do you mean God owns my swing?" "Yes." "Does God own the grass and the bushes?" "Yes." "Does God own the pricker bush too?" "Yes." "Well, Mommy, what does Jesus want with a pricker bush?"

   Psalm 50:1-12 is also useful in demonstrating the extent of God's ownership.

2. *Psalm 23.* As a family, memorize Psalm 23. This outstanding psalm is not often used to explain stewardship. However, it is the supreme example of how well God *takes care of* his people. God is our *model*. He makes us lie down; he restores us; he guides us; he removes our fear; he comforts us; he anoints us; he fills our cups to overflowing; and he makes goodness and love our guardians until we reach our eternal home. We cannot find a better model of one who *takes care of* people, and "taking care of" is a major

aspect of stewardship. Here we find a perfect lesson in modeling biblical stewardship.

3. *"This Is My Father's World."* Sing this well-known hymn as a family. Then talk about some of the following questions: What kind of ears do we need to hear about God's ownership? Why do some people miss all the beauty God has created? Why don't we need to worry when stewardship seems hard and it seems that selfish people are getting richer? What (how much or how little) does God trust us with? What does this "trust" suggest about God's employing us as stewards? Why, the writer asks, should my heart be sad? Or shouldn't it?

4. *"All Things Bright and Beautiful."* You can sing this song as a family and use it to teach that God is Creator and Owner of everything and everyone. Suggesting that the children color or draw pictures of some of the items in the song will help reinforce the idea.

5. *Thanksgiving.* As part of your family devotions, talk about the many things for which we are thankful to God. Then

thank God together for the many people, places, things, and other blessings God gives us.

6. *"The Young Look."* Read Joanne DeJonge's "The Young Look" (found in THE BANNER, the weekly publication of the Christian Reformed Church) to or with the children. Each story is creatively written about some aspect of the natural world around us (animals, bugs, plants, and more), and will demonstrate to children the greatness of our Creator and Owner. God takes care of even the tiniest creatures.

7. *News Stories.* The mass media—television, newspapers, and magazines—very frequently run stories about the environment: air, water, and land pollution, and wasted resources—much of it caused by our greed, especially in North America. Read or watch appropriate news stories with your children or bring up the topic at the dinner table. These will provide stark examples of what happens when God's creatures do not exercise stewardship over the resources we have been given.

Case Studies

As you talk about each case listed here, try to answer the following four questions:

- What stewardship issues are involved here, if any?
- How can I instruct my children through what I say?
- How can I instruct my children through what I do?
- How can I instruct my children through what I have them do?

1. Your kids have circled numerous items (primarily toys) that they want for Christmas in the "Wishbook" catalog.

2. Your son loses his ten-speed bike because he forgot to lock it up when he left it outside the mall. He begs you for a new one and promises to lock it up from now on.

3. Your thirteen-year-old son has a regular income from his paper route, and you think he should make a pledge during Mission Emphasis Week. He protests that you already expect him to put half of his earnings away for college and that if he has to give to the church it will take forever to save enough for a new stereo.

4. Your high-school-aged daughter tells you that all of her friends are wearing the latest designer jeans. The jeans cost twenty dollars more per pair than the ones you planned to buy for her. She tells you that she is going to be socially "out of it" without the right pair.

5. Your daughter has just been married. She and her husband are working, but they haven't managed to save much. They approach you for a down payment on a new three-bedroom ranch they have their eye on in the suburbs.

Think, Pray, and Do

Think

1. In teaching children to be cost-conscious and encouraging them to plan and save, are we at the same time encouraging penny-pinching and hoarding? Why or why not? Does the Bible address the subject of hoarding? How? Should we discourage the practice?

2. What do your children see in your giving? Carefully evaluate how, how much, and for what you give. How much and what kind of an example do your children see? What can you improve in your own example to better teach your children the meaning of biblical stewardship?

Pray

1. Read the Meditation on pages 116-118.

2. Pray for wisdom in teaching children the importance and joy of giving.

Do

1. Review the suggestions for teaching stewardship on pages 107-113 of the Reflection section in this chapter. See if you can add an idea or two of your own to each list.

2. Your next group session will focus on the question "Where do we go from here?" During the week, think about that question and jot down some ideas of ways in which you might respond to what you've learned in these sessions— both as individuals and as a congregation.

Meditation

Meditation: Teaching Children

". . . and a little child will lead them."
—Isaiah 11:6

It is much more important to raise children than it is to raise cash. Parents are rightfully concerned about "Train(ing) a child in the way he should go," so that "when he is old he will not turn from it" (Prov. 22:6). And in fact God has directed parents to this task, saying "Teach them [My commandments] to your children, talking about them when you sit at home and when you walk along the road, when you lie down and when you get up. Write them [the commandments] on the doorframes of your houses and on your gates" (Deut. 11:19-20).

Today, children don't often sit at home with their parents, nor, perhaps, do many parents have time to sit at home with their children. Today's parents probably take fewer walks with their children than did the Hebrews, who walked to the fields to tend their sheep, fetch water, and gather kindling. Neither are God's commandments written under the street address numbers on a parent's house.

Does God's command still apply? Yes. Christian parents today take seriously the command to teach their children God's ways. Parents are so serious about teaching their children that if they can possibly afford to do so they spend thousands of dollars to insure that their children receive a God-centered education. Parents, consciously and subconsciously, are always "teaching children."

On the other hand, how often do parents look at and listen to their children as "teaching-children"? Children can and do teach adults—provided, of course, adults are listening and willing to learn. I think of the Andersons:

> They had just purchased a new refrigerator. They placed the old one in the basement, intending to transfer it to their summer cottage as a spare refrigerator for pop and other extras. The refrigerator was in good condition, but it did not have an ice-cube-making mechanism.
>
> Several weeks later the telephone rang while the family was eating dinner. When Dad (a deacon)

returned to the table, he mentioned that the caller was Mrs. Burke, a single mother with two little ones. Her refrigerator had given out. The repairman told her it would be very expensive to repair it. "Besides," the repairman had said, "something else may go wrong tomorrow." What should she do?

Before Dad could add that he intended to refer the request to the deacons, three-year-old Robin said, "I know, Dad. You can give her the one in the basement." The next day Mr. Anderson delivered the refrigerator to Mrs. Burke.

A little child will lead them.

Little children can be selfish little tyrants, true. The two-year-old isn't usually the most generous individual in the room. And the three-year-old will fight for what is his or hers. Yet innocent children can teach adults. Jesus said, "I praise you, Father, Lord of heaven and earth, because you have hidden these things from the wise and learned, and revealed them to little children. Yes, Father, for this was your good pleasure" (Matt. 11:25). Jesus did not mean that children are able to comprehend all the truths that adult Christians find precious. Rather, Jesus wants adults to be childlike: innocent, trusting, accepting, and always learning. A little girl isn't afraid to jump from a high spot because she knows her father will catch her.

A little child will lead them.

A little girl, sitting in a large church and looking up at a huge painting of Jesus on the arched ceiling above the organ, said to her grandma, "Grandma, do you know who that is up there? That's God, and he made the whole works!" Not a smattering of doubt!

A little child will lead them.

The God-inspired poet wrote, "From the lips of children and infants you have ordained praise" (Ps. 8:2). If you have listened to little children pray at the dinner table, you will know how long is the list of things for which they thank and praise God.

A little child will lead them.

When the disciples wanted to know who would be the greatest in the kingdom of heaven, Jesus called a little one and had him stand in the circle. Jesus said to the gathered group, "I tell you the truth, unless you change and become like little children, you will never enter the kingdom of heaven. Therefore, whoever humbles himself like this child is the greatest in the kingdom of heaven" (Matt. 18:2-4). He also said, "Let the little children come unto me, and do not hinder them, for the kingdom of heaven belongs to such as these" (Matt. 19:14).

A little child will lead them.

There is something about children that we adults need to learn from. As we teach them, we must let them also teach us.

Prayer

Take my life and let it be
consecrated, Lord, to thee.
Take my moments and my days;
let them flow in endless praise.

Take my silver and my gold;
not a mite would I withhold.
Take my intellect and use
every power as thou shalt choose.

Take my will and make it thine;
it shall be no longer mine.
Take my heart—it is thine own;
it shall be thy royal throne.

Take my love; my Lord I pour
at thy feet its treasure store.
Take myself and I will be
ever, only, all for thee.

Amen.

7

A Call to Action: Where Do We Go from Here?

Obedience

Give me understanding, and I will keep your law
and obey it with all my heart.
                    —Psalm 119:34

[Jesus] replied, "Blessed rather are those who hear the word of God
and obey it."
                    —Luke 11:28

Jesus replied, "If anyone loves me, he will obey my teaching."
                    —John 14:23

God's Grace

From the fullness of his grace we have all received one blessing
after another. For the law was given though Moses; grace and
truth came through Jesus Christ.
                    —John 1:16-17

But God demonstrates his own love for us in this: While we were
still sinners, Christ died for us . . . . [God's] gift . . . came by the
grace of the one man, Jesus Christ . . . . how much more will
those who receive God's abundant provision of grace and of the
gift of righteousness reign in life through the one man, Jesus
Christ.
                    —Romans 5:8, 15, 17

Thankfulness

I will give thanks to the LORD because of his righteousness.
                    —Psalm 7:17

Worship the LORD with gladness; come before him with joyful
songs.
                    —Psalm 100:2

Case Study: Jenison, Michigan

Rev. Robert Heerspink, Jenison, Michigan, taught the *Firstfruits* series to the 100+-family church of which he is pastor. He modified and adapted each session to meet the needs of his church's education program.

While the study was going on, the council wrestled with ways of improving congregational stewardship. They met twice with the FIRSTFRUITS staff from the Barnabas Foundation to talk about direction and to pinpoint areas where change in church structure would be helpful. Rev. Heerspink also preached a four-sermon series on biblical stewardship. "I did not begin with the premise that I had all the answers to stewardship questions," he notes. "I said to myself, 'Let's learn; let's discover together,' and that's exactly what happened as we learned and discovered new truths from God's Word."

While it is always difficult to establish cause and effect, the church achieved several stewardship goals in the months following the *Firstfruits* series. For the first time in several years, Cottonwood Heights CRC was able to pay denominational and classical quotas in full. Also, at the annual congregational meeting that followed their study, a building addition plan submitted to the congregation by the council was soundly *defeated!* Why? Because it was too expensive or extravagant? No. The congregation felt that the proposed expansion needed to be more visionary—even if it cost more. Months later members approved a more expensive building addition.

Excerpts from forty-nine evaluations indicate that the course was very effective in teaching biblical stewardship and joyful giving. Two-thirds of those responding indicated that the course had taught them new insights. (See "Sources of Information" p. 132, for information on receiving more details from Rev. Heerspink's program.)

1. If you were to write a similar case study of your congregation six months from now, what would you like it to say?

2. Rev. Heerspink's church showed their change in attitude about stewardship through their attitude about and action on the new building project. Where would you like to *see* changed attitudes in your congregation? In what ways can you visibly grow in your giving?

3. What part should your minister and council/consistory play in educating the congregation about stewardship? For example, should your pastor preach a series of sermons on giving, as Rev. Heerspink did?

4. Together study one or both of the two lists that follow: Personal Action or Group Action. Add some of your own ideas to the lists. Then take time to fill out the Quit-Claim Deed and the Personal Pledge Card in Appendix 7a and 7b in this book. Prepare to talk about your discussion and your plans with the larger group.

Personal Action

Reflect on the following personal suggestions and/or the group suggestions on pages 128-130 before you fill out the Quit-Claim Deed and the Personal Pledge Card (Appendix 7a and 7b). See if you can expand the list with some ideas of your own.

A. *Sharpened consciousness*. Pray and pledge that your consciousness about lifestyle may remain sharp. Fill out the Quit-Claim Deed, turning all of your property over to God. Decide to apply biblical stewardship to specific matters such as buying on credit and buying a new item when the item in use is not worn out.

B. *Level of lifestyle*. Pray that you will remain conscious of the *level* of your lifestyle. Pledge to scrutinize closely *all* purchases or activities that subtly increase your cost of living. In the early 1990s Nintendo games, VCRs, recreational vehicles, exotic or expensive vacations, high-tech sports equipment, and more serve as "state of the art" possessions that are becoming increasingly common in North American society. Tomorrow newer inventions, trends, and fads will replace those we "can't do without" today.

C. *Special ways to give*. A generous heart often looks for creative ways to give. Consider some of the following: Give away the money you save by using coupons. Save your pennies, nickels, or dimes for specific causes. Add "Charity" to your entertainment by "buying" her a ticket or a dinner out and giving this amount to a favorite charity. Give 1 percent of the money you spend for vacation each year to a cause of your choice. Share your own ideas with the group.

D. *Adoption of an agency*. Select an agency that helps to feed and clothe the poor and tries to find shelter for the homeless in your area. Get from that agency the name of one individual you may help. Determine with that person his or her needs and talk about how you can best help that individual overcome those needs and become a contributing member of society. This may involve time as well as money. The more you can learn about *how best* to help someone, the better your help will succeed.

E. *God or mammon?* Change your focus or attitude about money. Perhaps you are one whose life has centered around money. This series of sessions may have helped you see more clearly that money is a *resource*, every penny of which belongs to God. The true battle, says Philip Yancey in *Christianity Today*, "is a spiritual deliverance from money's power." "Whom do you serve," Jesus asked, "God or mammon (money)?" Money is useless unless it is spent. Decide to concentrate simply on "How will I *use* this resource?" and "Am I accumulating more than I need on earth?"

F. *Resolutions.* Make a personal pledge to grow in biblical stewardship in several ways. View it as a challenge. You may also wish to share periodically with others who have also resolved to grow in stewardship. Sharing your successes and failures with one another will help strengthen your resolve. The sharing could include a time of prayer and devotions to strengthen your stewardly response.

G. *Personal or family budget.* Plan to keep a weekly or monthly personal or family budget in which your gift to God and your savings (no matter how small) are top priorities. (See Personal Budget Sheet, Appendix 3a.)

H. *Special choice.* Think of some clothes or a piece of clothing that you planned to buy and for which you have or are saving money. Decide to sacrifice that item and give the money to a specific congregational or denominational ministry.

I. *Personal relationship.* Establish, by mail or in person, a personal relationship with a teacher, nurse, doctor, minister, or other worker who has dedicated his or her life to a local or foreign mission field or to a sacrificial service ministry. Become personally involved with prayer and with gifts to the work in which that person is engaged.

J. *Teaching your children.* Involve each child in all family stewardship activities—particularly the giving that is tied to very visible causes—and make giving a family project.

K. *Debt reduction.* Make a list of your current debts (not including your mortgage payments) and the payments required to eliminate each of them. Resolve to make no major or unnecessary purchases until you have eliminated your debts.

L. *Prayer*. Ask God daily to increase your knowledge of, sensitivity to, and execution of acts of stewardship, until they become a well-integrated part of your lifestyle. God does answer our prayers.

M. *Informed giving*. Get from your deacons a list of the special offerings for the next quarter. During the week prior to each special offering, discuss it with your family, especially the children, and seek more information if you need it. Decide as a family how much you will give, and ask the

Better stewardship means we lower our lifestyle, don't you think?

Sure!

children to consider how much they will give. If the cause is not one you believe you should support, discuss this too with the children and furnish sound reasons for not participating.

N. *Mail solicitations*. Do not automatically throw out the dozens of requests you receive for funds. Accumulate them. Identify the causes represented. Discuss with the family, especially teenagers and young adults who are earning money, the strengths and weaknesses of solicitation of funds by mail. Discuss the importance of knowing the agencies, organizations, and ministries you choose to support.

O. *Television's lure*. Television programs display requests for funds, usually through commercials or through evangelistic or worship services that revolve around a particular, popular evangelist. Note the following: the causes represented; the vigor of the appeal to the emotions; your inability to determine how financially responsible the causes are; how much time the program gives to fund raising; what the funds are used for. Discuss the fact that as biblical stewards we are responsible for the way the money we give is used.

P. *Discretionary funds*. From these funds (which are not allocated to set expenses or savings), set aside a specified weekly or monthly amount to have ready for giving to people who suffer from catastrophes such as floods, fires, tornados, earthquakes, and the like. Be sure to channel the gift through a trustworthy agency about which you are well informed.

Q. *Christmas giving*. With your family, consciously plan to make your next Christmas a celebration of Jesus' *birthday*. Celebrate in a manner that resembles the way your family celebrates other birthdays. Children become very excited about their own or other family members' birthdays. Channel that enthusiasm and creativity into celebrating Jesus' birthday as well.

R. *Financial planning*. Plan now to call the Barnabas Foundation and ask them to help you exercise responsible biblical stewardship in preparing your will or a living trust. This information is available by writing or calling the Barnabas Foundation, 15127 S. 73rd Ave., Suite G, Orland Park, IL 60462. (708) 532-3444.

Group Action

You may want to join with others in your group and consider some of the following activities:

A. *Parental support group*. Decide to meet regularly to discuss the needs and wants of your children and to talk about ways of wisely using the gift of making money that God has given to many of you. Discussions may include topics like the cost and appropriateness of name-brand and special clothing, accessories, entertainment equipment (TV, telephone, Nintendo), vacations, or whatever things children feel they "cannot do without." Such a group can help parents (and their children) deal wisely with the peer pressure brought about by today's materialism and consumerism.

The following questions may help in organizing a support group:

1. How many families would provide an optimum number to deal with such financial issues?

2. Should all the families be in approximately the same income bracket or should incomes reach across several brackets?

3. Should children—at least the teenagers—meet with the group?

4. Will the decisions made be binding or only suggestive?

5. How often will the group meet?

B. *Financial planning*. Invite a financial planner to speak to your group on ways to develop basic budgeting and family bookkeeping skills. Perhaps one of your deacons could do this. Or, members of the group might wish to serve as counselors for people who find it hard to budget their money. By doing so, they could help others to become more systematic in their planning, acquisition, spending, and saving, while reinforcing the ideas learned in this course in their own minds.

C. *Church finances*. Request a meeting with deacon representatives to learn how deacons determine the church's annual budget. A review of the budget will show you how congregational priorities are reflected in sums spent in ministry and outreach. Discuss with the deacons your concerns about stewardship in and of the church. Discuss various concepts of giving (per family, percentage, graduated percentage, faith-promise, etc.); ask why the method your church uses was chosen. Perhaps you can convince the deacons to share this information with the congregation so that everyone may become more conscious of biblical stewardship.

You may also wish to learn more about the ministries you support through your denominational budget. See letter E under "Sources of Information" for people you can contact to find out more information about the communal ministry of the CRC.

D. *Stewardship committee.* Ask the council to appoint a congregational stewardship committee and mandate them to keep biblical stewardship issues alive in your church.

This committee would be separate from the church's finance committee. Its task would be to plan regularly scheduled activities on stewardship issues, including, perhaps, a "Stewardship Sunday" at regular intervals.

The following questions may help you establish such a committee:

1. What will be the task of the stewardship committee?

2. Will membership include one or more deacons? Elders? The minister?

3. Will this committee work with the deacons or the finance committee in preparing the annual budget?

4. Will this committee be responsible for the continued teaching of stewardship in the church?

5. Will this committee be asked to prepare bulletin announcements for the church on stewardship issues?

E. *Encouraging the pastor.* Encourage your pastor to meet on a regular basis with the deacons to stress the *spiritual* nature of their work. Emphasize the point that biblical stewardship is a subject that needs to be more central in congregational life.

F. *Encouraging the deacons.* Encourage your deacons to take responsibility for regularly and effectively communicating to the congregation the aims, purposes, and needs of the organizations for which an offering, regular or special, is taken.

G. *Group support.* Decide to make personal resolutions to grow personally in biblical stewardship. Meet periodically with others who have made the same resolution. Share both your successes and your failures. These meeting times could include a time of prayer and devotions to strengthen each person's efforts to become a better steward.

H. *Educating church officials.* Decide to focus on a way for the group to convey to the deacons, the elders, and the pastors, the principles, privilege, and challenge of biblical stewardship as an expression of gratitude.

I. *Sharing the series.* Decide to repeat this seven-session series with other groups, especially the young people of the church, and begin arrangements to make this effort.

J. *Joining special groups.* Decide to seek to learn more about and support the Christian Reformed World Relief Committee, which is not a quota-supported ministry. Or join organizations such as Bread for the World or the Association for Public Justice. All three organizations deal with questions closely related to the stewardship practices of the wealthy.

Sources of Information

Many materials are available to help the church continue its quest for better biblical stewardship. Following are some sources you may wish to pursue:

A. *Barnabas Foundation.* The function of the Barnabas Foundation is to assist all Christians in extending their lifelong pattern of good stewardship into their wills and estate plans. Its major method of meeting this goal is by presentations to groups of Christian adults on the topic of wills and estates. From a distinctly Christian perspective and in an entertaining and understandable manner, Barnabas representatives introduce the basic principles of long-range estate planning. Barnabas services are for everyone—not just the wealthy.

After each group presentation, Barnabas provides free consultation appointments to individuals and couples to help them meet personal and family stewardship goals. Barnabas does not perform the ensuing legal work, but does follow up these consultations by sending letters that summarize the individual family's situation. The individual or the family then take the letter to their local attorney for translation into appropriate legal documents. Barnabas often provides the professionals with specimen forms and documents to assist them in completing their work.

Because all of the Foundation's operating costs are covered by annual dues from member organizations, Barnabas representatives are able to meet with individuals without cost or obligation. Barnabas representatives do not solicit personal conferences; their visits result from individual requests.

The Barnabas Foundation is also a trustee of a number of charitable trusts and manages a philanthropic fund for the distribution of special gifts (such as appreciated properties) during the donor's lifetime. The staff also helps churches and organizations (such as local Christian Schools) to provide information on organizing and operating a foundation or an endowment fund.

To obtain more information or to schedule a meeting write to:

The Barnabas Foundation
15127 S. 73rd Avenue
Orland Park, IL 60462
Telephone: (708) 532-3444

B. *FIRSTFRUITS.* Teaching about and promoting the principles of biblical stewardship are functions of the FIRST-FRUITS program, the stewardship project of the Barnabas Foundation. One key area FIRSTFRUITS touches is that of the deacon's role, especially its challenge to teach the principles of biblical stewardship in an ongoing way. Materials offered by the project include the following:

1. What Is FIRSTFRUITS?
2. How to Deal with Delinquent Givers
3. Church Giving Profile—Stewardship Self-Study
4. Defining the Faith-Promise Offering
5. Sample Congregational Pledge Card
6. Principles of Financial Stewardship
7. Criteria Suggestions for Making Church Stewardship Decisions
8. Evaluation Forms for Church Stewardship

The above materials will be sent upon request. Write or call:

FIRSTFRUITS Stewardship Project
Barnabas Foundation
15127 South 73rd Avenue
Orland Park, IL 60462
Telephone: (708) 532-3444

C. *Report on successful teaching of* Firstfruits. Rev. Robert Heerspink, Jenison, Michigan, taught the seven-session *Firstfruits* program to a Christian Reformed Church of more than one hundred families, as explained in the case study in this chapter.

For information and materials, write to:

Rev. Robert Heerspink
8215 Ash Dr.
Jenison, MI 49428

D. *Love Inc. (Love in the name of Christ)* An excellent interdenominational stewardship education program is in place at Love Inc., Ottawa County, Michigan. Counselors are trained to assist people in meeting immediate and long-term needs in a biblically based stewardship program. The process works in the following manner:

1. Individuals either come to Love Inc. on their own, or they are referred to the organization by a pastor, a church, or an organization in Ottawa county that sees the individual's need for help.
2. A screening process determines whether the need is real, whether the need is a recurring problem, and what the overall status of the client is. The counselor needs to determine whether the individual or family is already a case client at another agency, since Love Inc. must rule out the possibility of multi-agency assistance programs if it is going to work with a client. To avoid duplication of relief and help, Love Inc. keeps a record of all applications for assistance.
3. Love Inc. then finds help for the qualified applicant at other agencies or churches. Although the Love Inc. program does give emergency assistance when such help is needed, its role is to be a "clearing house" for meeting needs. It generally refers cases to supporting churches and agencies. If a need for clothing exists, Love Inc. gives the person written authorization to visit a local church "Clothes Closet." If a need for food exists, it authorizes the client to visit one of five church "Community Pantries."
4. If the client requesting help is a member of one of the supporting churches, Love Inc. contacts the church to arrange an assistance plan.

The key to the Love Inc. program is its success in helping people break the "need cycle." The question it asks each client is "How will you change your present situation?" It recognizes that clients must commit themselves to trying to reverse their present need situation.

It is imperative that clients receiving more than one-time help submit to budget counseling and personal finance training. Budget counseling is done on a one-on-one basis by trained, volunteer counselors, who use both videos and lectures. Strong action may be necessary: Sometimes the counselor may literally take over the client's checkbook for a time. At other times, counselors unceremoniously cut up the client's credit cards. The goal is always to help clients manage and control their finances.

Sometimes clients incur debt to Love Inc. during the financial training phase. In such cases, Love Inc. requires these clients to sign a legally unenforceable pledge, promising to make monthly payments of 10 percent of their gross income until the debt is paid. This system is intended to help them reestablish themselves and at the same time initiate a "tithing model."

Jacob Mol, a Love Inc. steering committee member who is familiar with the group's relief approach, urges all churches to establish similar educational assistance programs for members who presently cannot manage their God-given resources. Mol notes that our churches have too many members who give little or nothing to the church budget.

E. *The Christian Reformed Church Finance Coordinator.* Consider devising a means for your local church to provide better information on the exciting worldwide ministries that are made possible by quota, offerings, and gifts provided by members of your congregation. Invite members of your group to volunteer to do the following:

1. Contact the denominational financial coordinator. The coordinator will send information on the denominational quota system and other related financial matters. Direct your request to the denominational financial coordinator, Harry Vander Meer, at 2850 Kalamazoo Ave., Grand Rapids, MI 49560.

2. Contact your classical or regional representatives. All agencies supported by quota funds have classical representatives.

3. Call your denominational agency and ask for the person responsible for church relations, promotions, and public information.

4. Contact the Christian Reformed World Relief Committee, a non-quota agency that works to relieve world hunger and to provide assistance for victims of disasters. CRWRC offers resources that help deacons fulfill the call to inspire faithful stewardship in the congregation. Information provided by resource staff in one of the many regional diaconal conferences across the United States is available by calling 1-800-848-5818.

5. Ask the deacons to establish a "Ministry Moment" before each offering. During these "moments" someone from the council or congregation can briefly describe the work of the agency supported by the offering. Such information will enable givers to understand

the causes they are supporting and to make better judg-
ments about how much they want to contribute.

F. *Crown Ministries.* Resources to help individuals and families in personal budgeting are available from Crown
Ministries, 530 Crown Oak Centre Drive, Longwood,
Florida 32750 (Phone: 407-331-6000). The materials are
available in either a cash budgeting system or in a check-
ing account budgeting setup. A text with the accompanying workbooks is available for $42.00 from the above
address.

G. *Net Results Resource Center.* This center, a part of the
National Evangelistic Association, has an excellent program called "The *Consecration Sunday Stewardship
Program*, written by Herb Miller. The program seeks to
make church members better stewards, to help them
accept a sacred partnership with God, and to encourage
them to give systematically and proportionately of their
income.

All materials needed for the program (sample letters,
giving cards, and posters) are provided with detailed
instructions to help the church make the *Consecration
Sunday Program* successful. It is suggested that financial
commitment be made part of the worship service and that
there be *no calling on members in their homes for a pledge.*
The program has had success in both small and large congregations.

A complete outline of the program, including all necessary forms, is available for $28.00 from

Net Results Resource Center
5001 Avenue, North
Lubbock, Texas 79412-2917
Tel. (706) 762-8904, or Fax (806) 762-8873.

H. Master Your Money *Program.* In reviewing the literature
that is available on Christian stewardship, we have found
no single item as comprehensive and practical, and yet
biblically sound, as the video-lecture program *Master Your
Money.* This program, developed by Christian financial
advisor Ron Blue and the Walk Through the Bible
Ministries, is heartily endorsed by FIRSTFRUITS, the
stewardship project of the Barnabas Foundation.

This six-part video, with accompanying student workbook, provides a strong biblical perspective on the acquisition, use, management, and distribution of money. The program can greatly benefit every Christian Reformed person and family.

The major theme of the video series is teaching people how to free up their resources to help build God's kingdom on earth through the church and supporting agencies. It is a real-life, hands-on, practical guide to giving, saving, spending, and managing money—all from a clear, biblical perspective. By using prayer and Scripture to establish financial faith goals, church members will learn ways to commit more in faith-giving and will see their dollars go farther when they are given to God first.

The program is suited for an adult education program where the leader may not feel comfortable "teaching" materials that deal with finances and money. The program can stand on its own if the outline is followed carefully. However, we have experienced some difficulty with the time (45-50 minutes) necessary to view the videos. In a one-hour class session, the video program leaves little time for meaningful discussion. As a result, you may want to consider one of the following variations:

1. Use the video in one session and discuss it in the next session.
2. View one half of the video in one session and follow it with discussion; use the second half with discussion in your next session.
3. Show one half of the video in two consecutive sessions, followed by discussion in a third session. (This format provides a nine-week format that has been used with some success.)

The program itself is *entertaining*. Broadcast-quality dramas are an integral part of each session and will capture participants' interest and make each lesson personal and relevant.

The lessons are also *practical*. Course workbooks provide reliable notes and financial worksheets needed to organize and plan one's finances. An effective strategy for getting out of debt *for good* is provided. Most importantly, the program is *spiritual*. Each lesson shares biblical principles God has given to help us become better stewards of the earth's resources.

Whether you are single, newly married, raising a family, or have been married for many years, *Master Your Money* can be a great help to you as you seek to be a good steward of what God has given you.

For more information, call or contact:

FIRSTFRUITS
15127 S. 73rd Avenue, Suite G
Orland Park, IL 60462
Telephone: (708) 532-3444

If you wish to order, please write or call

CRC Publications
2850 Kalamazoo Avenue, SE
Grand Rapids, MI 49560
1-800-333-8300

or

CRC Publications
P.O. Box 5070
Burlington, ON L7R 3Y8
1-800-263-4252

Prayer

O Lord God of Israel,
there is no God like you in heaven above,
or on earth below—
you who keep your covenant of love with your servants,
who continue wholeheartedly in your way.
You have kept your promise to your servant David, my father;
with your mouth you have promised and
with your hand you have fulfilled it—
as it is today.
Our Father in heaven,
we are filled with gratitude,
for the fulfillment of all your promises.
Help us now and forever
to gratefully live
as wise and loving stewards
of your gifts to us.
For Jesus' sake,
Amen.

Evaluation

Firstfruits: Managing the Master's Money

We hope you enjoyed this series of lessons on stewardship. We would appreciate your help in evaluating and improving this course. Please circle the appropriate numbers, 1-5 (1 = very poor; 5 = excellent).

1. The lessons are biblically based.   1 2 3 4 5

2. The lessons helped change my attitudes
   about giving for kingdom ministries.   1 2 3 4 5

3. The lessons have helped me change my
   giving patterns.   1 2 3 4 5

   In what specific ways?

4. How helpful did you find each of the following course
   components?

   Bible Study   1 2 3 4 5

   Case Studies   1 2 3 4 5

   Group discussion   1 2 3 4 5

   Reflections (textbook readings)   1 2 3 4 5

   Charts and Graphs (Appendix)   1 2 3 4 5

   Think, Pray, and Do   1 2 3 4 5

   Meditations   1 2 3 4 5

   Cartoons   1 2 3 4 5

   Bibliography   1 2 3 4 5

5. How would you rate the course's coverage of the following topics?

God is owner of all.	1 2 3 4 5
Stewardship is God's management system.	1 2 3 4 5
Managing our money	1 2 3 4 5
Financial planning	1 2 3 4 5
Communal giving	1 2 3 4 5
Teaching stewardship	1 2 3 4 5
A call to stewardship	1 2 3 4 5

What topics would you like to see covered or covered more fully?

6. How many of the seven sessions did you attend? Which ones did you attend?

7. To which age group do you belong? _____ Under 25, _____ 26-30, _____ 31-45, _____ 46-60, _____ Over 60

If you desire any follow-up information from the Barnabas Foundation, please indicate the kind of information you wish and include your name and address.

Follow-up desired:
Name: _____
Church: _____
City, State/Province: _____

Please return forms to:
FIRSTFRUITS Stewardship Project
Barnabas Foundation
15127 S. 73rd Ave., Suite G
Orland Park, IL 60462

Bibliography

The following resources have been selected from a long list of available materials, most of which are available at local Christian bookstores or directly from the publishers. Your church library may wish to order some of these resources as a way of assisting members of your congregation in honoring biblical principles in the acquisition, management, use, and distribution of the money that God has entrusted to them.

Atlas, Liane W. *Financial Planning For Widowhood: What Every Wife Should Know Now*. Washington, D.C.: Fintapes, Inc. Cassette tape.
> Acknowledging the reality that 10 out of 12 married women will be widows, the speaker narrates a step-by-step program for becoming prepared to deal with some of the practical issues of life that women often leave to their husbands. The cassette also includes a discussion entitled "Dollars and Sense: Financial Advice You Can Listen To." This cassette is available from Fintapes, Inc., Suite 700, 1629 K Street NW, Washington, D.C. 20006. (202) 337-3636.

Berghoef, G., and L. De Koster. *The Deacon's Handbook: A Manual of Stewardship*. Grand Rapids, MI: Library Press, 1980.
> *The Deacon's Handbook* is an excellent resource for teaching biblical stewardship. It should be required reading for every church officebearer and for anyone who is concerned with stewardship of the material resources God has given us.

Blue, Ronald. *The Debt Squeeze: How Your Family Can Become Debt Free*. Pomona, CA: Focus on the Family Publishing, 1989.
> Ron Blue explains what motivates us to borrow and how lenders entice us to take on debilitating debt. He shows the reader how to beat the debt squeeze and find real financial freedom.

Blue, Ronald. *Master Your Money; Discovering God's Principles for Financial Freedom*. Nashville, TN: Thomas Nelson, Inc., 1990.
> Ron Blue's work in financial planning has helped today's Christians realize the Bible's timeless teaching

on stewardship. His book provides sound insights on financial management that will help readers work toward financial freedom. The text is illustrated by detailed charts and worksheets. Available from CRC Publications; 1-800-333-8300 (US), 1-800-263-4252 (CDA).

Blue, Ronald. *Master Your Money Video Training Series.* Atlanta, GA: Ronald Blue & Co. Videocassette series.
This six-part video series has trained thousands of Christians to become better stewards of their finances by applying biblical principles along with sound financial wisdom. This series is ideal for church group, seminar, and family settings. Available from Ronald Blue & Co., 1100 Johnson Ferry Road NE, Suite 600, Atlanta, Georgia, 30342, or from CRC Publications; call 1-800-333-8300 (US), 1-800-263-4252 (CDA). Also available for loan rhrough TRAVARCA film and video library; call 1-800-688-7221.

Burkett, Larry. *Answers to Your Family's Financial Questions.* Pomona, CA: Focus on the Family Publishing, 1987.
Larry Burkett's many years of experience as a Christian financial counselor are reflected in this book that provides biblically based answers to today's real questions. This is an excellent resource for individuals and families, both young and mature, in all seasons of life.

Burkett, Larry. *What The Bible Says About Money: A Topical Concordance Related to Money.* Brentwood, TN: Wolgemuth and Hyatt Publishers, Inc., 1989.
In a single volume, Larry Burkett compiles all the references to money that are found in the Bible. This book is an excellent topical and cross-reference resource for the serious student.

Burkett, Larry. *The How-to's of Family Financial Management; How To Get Out of Debt; Financial Seasons of a Marriage; Your Money: A Biblical Perspective.* Pomona, CA: Focus on the Family. Cassette tapes.
These practical audio discussions between financial planner Larry Burkett and Dr. James Dobson are available from Focus on the Family, Pomona, California, 91799.

Dayton, Howard L. *Your Money: Frustration or Freedom?* (The Biblical Guide to Earning, Saving, Spending, Investing and Giving). Wheaton, IL: Tyndale House Publishers, Inc., 1979.

Dayton, in his review of the extensive biblical admonitions concerning our use of money, may convince his readers that the problem of money is more than just not getting enough of it. It involves mind and spirit and is a matter of freedom that is of concern to God.

De Vos, Karen. "Stewardship," a topical booklet, one part of the *In His Service* series. Grand Rapids, MI: CRC Publications, 1987.

This booklet deals with the subject of stewardship in the church. Included in this booklet are practical suggestions for teaching stewardship to members and helping those who have been delinquent in their support of ministry. Available from CRC Publications, 2850 Kalamazoo Ave. SE, Grand Rapids, MI 49560, or call 1-800-333-8300.

Ellul, Jacques. *Money and Power.* Downer's Grove, IL: InterVarsity Press, 1984.

Ellul traces biblical attitudes toward wealth from Old Testament sacramentalism through New Testament renunciation. He challenges Christians to live by the law of grace rather than by the law of the marketplace. In contrast to the many resources that focus on debt and its negative effect on financial freedom (a major preoccupation of Christian money managers today), Ellul deals with our universal dependence on money.

Getz, Gene A. *Real Prosperity: Biblical Principles of Material Possessions.* Chicago, IL: Moody Press, 1990.

Real Prosperity offers guidance about sacrificial giving, aiding the poor, caring financially for family members, and avoiding our bondage to materialism. This practical advice, given in an easy-to-read format, is straight from the Scriptures.

Hybels, Bill. *Christians in the Marketplace.* Wheaton, IL: Scripture Press Publications, Inc., 1988.

Bill Hybels presents practical and biblical answers to pertinent questions about work, leisure, money, and authority. He warns his readers about the dangers of being a Christian consumer in a materialistic society, and exposes the subtleties that Satan uses to disarm those who attempt to live a Christian life. *Christians in the Marketplace* is also available in a two-cassette audio format from the same publisher.

MacGregor, Malcolm, with S.G. Baldwin. *Your Money Matters.* Minneapolis, MN: Bethany House Publishers, 1980. This practical reader about dollars and sense is written by a C.P.A. who has a firm grip on both the meaning of money and the Word from the Lord. The chapters on budgeting and financial planning and on training our children in money matters are highly recommended.

Sine, T., *Why Settle For More And Miss The Best?* Waco, TX: Word Books, Inc. 1987. This book, a collection of scholarly insights gathered from the Wheaton '83 conference on the nature and mission of the church, reflects on the "lifestyles" issue in practicing good biblical stewardship. Good additional reading on the subject of wealth and its challenges.

Small Group Financial Study Guide and Practical Application Workbook. Longwood, FL: Crown Ministries. This program trains people to be financially faithful so that they can know Christ more intimately and be freed financially to serve him. In this intensive program, Scripture memorization and a practical application are daily homework requirements. Available from Crown Ministries, 530 Crown Oak Centre Drive, Longwood, Florida, 32750. Phone: (407) 331-6000.

Stewards Come In All Sizes, a Children and Youth Stewardship Resource. Louisville, KY: The Westminster Press/ John Knox Press. This stewardship education packet provides the materials necessary to incorporate children and youth into congregational stewardship programs. Made available by the Presbyterian Church (USA). Contact: Distribution Management Services, 100 Witherspoon St., Louisville, KY 40202-1396. (1-800-524-2612).

Stewardship and You. South Deerfield, MA: Channing L. Bete Co., Inc. This booklet will help church members find greater joy in living through giving. It is one in a series of booklets on stewardship, written for churches who desire to help their members reach their greatest potential as Christian stewards. Available from the Channing L. Bete Co., Inc., 200 State Road, South Deerfield, MA 01373-0200, or call toll-free for information and materials at 1-800-628-7733.

TRAVARCA *Film and Video Library.*
TRAVARCA provides an audiovisual library for the Christian Reformed Church in North America and the Reformed Church in America. The library offers excellent stewardship teaching resources for use in the church ministry. For more information, call TRAVARCA at 1-800-688-7221.

Willmer, W.K. *Money For Ministries: Biblical Guidelines for Giving and Asking.* Chicago, IL: Victor Books, 1989.
For those who support ministries with their money and for those who ask in the name of Christ, it is just as important to know *why* as it is to know *how* to provide and seek funds. Because the quality of financial support and asking should be different for Christian stewards, this book provides a practical and useful guide for biblical stewardship.

Yancey, Philip. *Confronting the Power of a Modern Idol.* Portland, OR: Multnomah Press, 1985. Monograph.
This short but strong essay describes the powerful force that money had on the author. The realization that he needed to come to terms with the Bible's strong statements about money is described in such a way that every Christian steward will benefit from it.

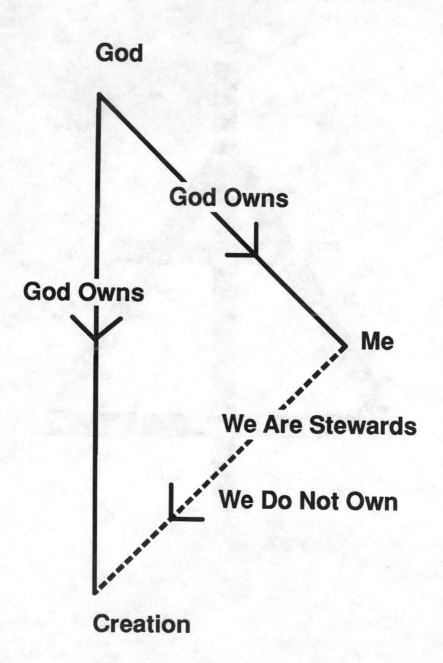

Personal Budget Sheet—Expenses

Fixed Expenses	Yearly
1. Church Budget,	
Contributions	_____
2. House	
a. Mortgage Payment	_____
b. Taxes and Assmts.	_____
c. Maintenance	_____
3. Utilities & Services	
a. Electricity	_____
b. Gas or Oil	_____
c. Water	_____
d. Sewer	_____
e. Garbage	_____
f. Telephone	_____
g. Cable TV	_____
h. Other	_____
4. Automobile (s)	
a. Payments	_____
b. Licenses	_____
5. Insurance	
a. Homeowners	_____
b. Life	_____
c. Medical	_____
d. Automobile	_____
6. Education	
a. Tuition	_____
b. Books & Fees	_____
7. Medical	
a. Doctor's Fees	_____
b. Dental & Orthodontia	_____
c. Medications	_____
8. Miscellaneous	
a. Newspapers & Magazines	_____
b. Music Lessons, etc.	_____
9. Christmas & Other Gifts	_____
10. Other	_____
TOTAL FIXED EXPENSES	_____
/ 48 weeks =	_____
FIXED WEEKLY EXPENSE	_____

Variable Expenses	Yearly
1. Groceries	
a. Home	_____
b. Restaurants	_____
c. Tobacco & Other	_____
2. Automobile (s)	
a. Gasoline	_____
b. Maintenance	_____
c. Repairs	_____
3. Recreation	
a. Movies	_____
b. Hobbies	_____
c. Vacations	_____
4. Clothing/Shoes	_____
5. Personal Care	
a. Hair Care	_____
b. Other Products	_____
6. Special Church Offerings	_____
7. Babysitters	_____
8. Credit Card Payments	_____
9. Other	_____
TOTAL VARIABLE EXPENSES	_____
/ 48 weeks =	_____
VARIABLE WEEKLY EXPENSE	_____

Deposit an amount equal to the "fixed weekly expense" into an account used only for making payments to fixed expenses.

Deposit an amount equal to the "variable weekly expense" into an account used for paying such expenses.

Record of Income, Expenses, and Savings

For the Month of _____ 19___

Income		Expenses			
Sources					
Employer (s)	_____	Contributions	_____	Personal Care	
	_____	Rent or Mortgage	_____	Barber	
	_____	Food		Beauty Parlor	_____
		Groceries	_____	Toiletry Items	_____
Child Support	_____	Eating Out	_____	Cosmetics	_____
		Tobacco	_____	Education	
General Assistance	_____	Beverages	_____	Tuition/Fees	_____
Alimony	_____	Telephone	_____	Books	_____
				Supplies	_____
Aid to Dependent	_____	Utilities		Recreation	
		Gas	_____	Movies	_____
Children	_____	Water	_____	Hobbies	_____
		Electric	_____	Bowling	_____
Social Security	_____	Sewer	_____	Vacations	_____
Income	_____	Garbage Removal	_____	Cable TV	_____
				Other	_____
Pension	_____	Furniture			
		Appliances	_____	Babysitting	_____
Disability Insurance	_____	Furnishings	_____	Miscellaneous	
		Television	_____	Home Insurance	_____
Food Stamps	_____	Stereo	_____	House Taxes	_____
		Furniture	_____	Gifts	_____
Other	_____			Newspapers	_____
		Clothing/Shoes	_____	Magazines	_____
		Cleaning/Laundering	_____	Other	_____
		Transportation		Unpaid Bills	
		Gas	_____	Finance Company	_____
		Insurance	_____	Medical	_____
		Bus	_____		
		Car Payments	_____	Other	_____
		Car Repair	_____		_____
		Medical Care			_____
		Physician	_____	Savings	
		Dentist	_____	Life Insurance	_____
		Counselor	_____	Savings Acc't	_____
		Medication	_____	Checking Acc't	_____
		Health Insurance	_____	Investments	_____

TOTAL INCOME $ _____   TOTAL EXPENSES $ _____

TOTAL INCOME SHOULD EQUAL TOTAL EXPENSES

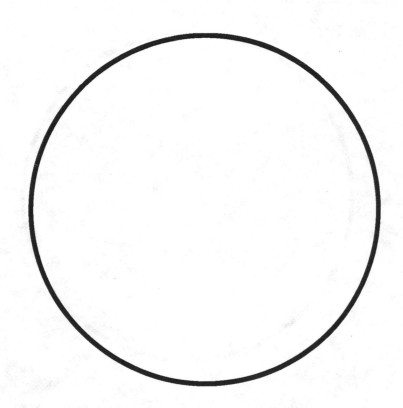

Spiritual World

— **Sunday Worship**
— **Values**
— **Spiritual**

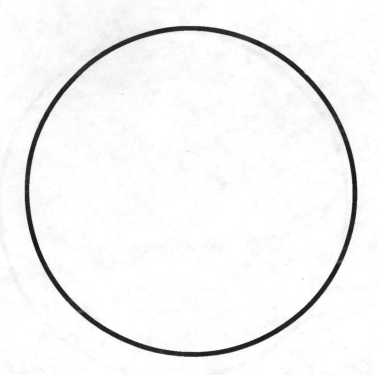

Material World

— **Daily Work**
— **Society (World)**
— **Material**

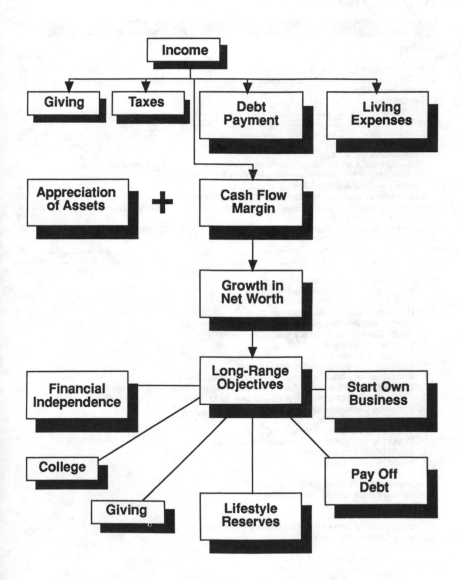

QUOTAS AND RECOMMENDED AGENCIES FOR 1992

Quotas

	Per family
Back to God Hour	$ 65.40
CRC-TV	24.35
Board of Home Missions	114.00
Calvin College	
Calvin Seminary	37.00
Chaplain Committee	9.35
CRC Publications	2.60
World Literature Ministries	2.00
Denominational Services	27.00

Institut Farel, $.50; Denominational Building Fund, $4.50; building operations, synodical expenses, funds for standing, service, and study committees, $22.00

Committee on Disability Concerns	2.00
Committee for Educational Assistance to Churches Abroad	1.25
Fund for Smaller Churches (includes quarterly subsidies and Continuing Education Fund)	2.00
Ministers' Pension Funds	38.50
Special Assistance and Moving Fund for Retired Ministers and Widows	2.75
Pastor-Church Relations Services	2.60
Synodical Committee on Race Relations	6.85
World Missions Committee	105.00

Recommended for one or more offerings
1. Back to God Hour—above-quota needs
   CRC TV—above-quota needs
2. Home Missions—above-quota needs
3. Calvin College—above-quota needs (per Schedule VIII)
4. Calvin Theological Seminary (per Schedule VIII)
   a. above-quota needs
   b. Revolving Loan Fund
5. Chaplain Committee—above-quota needs
6. Committee on Disability Concerns—above-quota needs
7. Committee for Educational Assistance to Churches Abroad—above-quota needs
8. Pastor Church Relations Services—above-quota needs
9. Synodical Committee on Race Relations
   a. above-quota needs
   b. Multiracial Student Scholarship Fund
10. World Literature Ministries—above-quota needs
11. World Missions Committee—above-quota needs
12. World Relief Committee

Denominationally Related Youth Agencies
Recommended for one or more offerings
1. Calvinettes
2. Calvinist Cadet Corps
3. Young Calvinist Armed Services Ministry
4. Young Calvinist Federation

Nondenominational Agencies for Financial Support

Recommended for financial support but not necessarily for one or more offerings

United States churches

Benevolent agencies
1. Bethany Christian Services
2. Bethesda PsycHealth System
3. Calvary Rehabilitation Center
4. Christian Health Care Center
5. Elim Christian School
6. International Aid Inc.
7. Luke Society, Inc.
8. Pine Rest Christian Hospital

Educational agencies
1. Center for Public Justice (formerly Association for Public Justice Education Fund)
2. Christian Schools International
3. Christian Schools International Foundation
4. Dordt College
5. International Theological Seminary
6. Rehoboth Christian School
7. Reformed Bible College
8. Roseland Christian School
9. Trinity Christian College
10. Westminster Theological Seminary Ministries (Philadelphia, PA, and Escondido, CA)
11. Worldwide Christian Schools

Miscellaneous agencies
1. American Bible Society
2. Faith, Prayer and Tract League
3. Friendship Foundation—USA
4. Gideons International—USA (Bible distribution only)
5. International Bible Society
6. Inter-Varsity Christian Fellowship—USA
7. Lord's Day Alliance
8. Metanoia Ministries
9. Reformed Ecumenical Council
10. Seminary Consortium for Urban Pastoral Education (SCUPE)
11. The Evangelical Literature League (TELL)
12. The Bible League
13. Wycliffe Bible Translators, Inc.(USA)

_____

_____

_____

_____

_____

_____

Comments
(Your Comments are Important)

Congregational Pledge Card

"Honor the LORD with your wealth, with the firstfruits of all your crops."
Proverbs 3:9

In gratitude to God for his many blessings, I/we intend to give, through the church, a planned financial gift for this year.

My/Our current weekly or monthly offering is_____.

My/Our stewardship intention for the coming year will be $_____ per (week, month) beginning today.

Signature (s) _____/_____
(This card expresses intention only and is not legally binding)

Please drop this card in the Offertory this Sunday or mail to the church office.

**My
Commitment
To God**

Giving to my
local church
helps me to fulfill
the commitment I
have made to God
for local and
worldwide
ministries.

My
Commitment
To God

Family

Local
Church

Classis/Regional

Denomination/World

"Therefore go and
make disciples of all
nations . . . and
surely I am with you
always, to the very
end of the age."
Matthew 28:20

Quit-Claim Deed

This Quit-Claim Deed, made the _____ day of _____ , 19 _____

FROM:

TO: The Lord

I (we) hereby transfer to the Lord the ownership of the following possessions:

Steward(s) of the possessions above:

Witnesses who will help hold me (us) accountable in the recognition of God's Ownership:

_____

_____

_____

_____

_____

_____

_____

_____

Personal Pledge

In gratitude to God,
I commit myself to the following
action steps in stewardship:

1. _____

_____

2. _____

_____

3. _____

_____

Name _____

Date _____